<u>Teaming with Life</u>

# How to Grow Your Own Tea at Home in Any Climate and 40 Food & Drink Recipes For Tea

Micah Bailey

© **Copyright 2021 - All rights reserved.**

The content contained within this book may not be reproduced, duplicated, or transmitted without direct written permission from the author or the publisher. Under no circumstances will any blame or legal responsibility be held against the publisher, or author, for any damages, reparation, or monetary loss due to the information contained within this book, either directly or indirectly.

Legal Notice:

This book is copyright protected. It is only for personal use. You cannot amend, distribute, sell, use, quote or paraphrase any part, or the content within this book, without the consent of the author or publisher.

Disclaimer Notice:

Please note the information contained within this document is for educational and entertainment purposes only. All effort has been executed to present accurate, up to date, reliable, complete information. No warranties of any kind are declared or implied. Readers acknowledge that the author is not engaged in the rendering of legal, financial, medical, or professional advice. The content within this book has been derived from various sources. Please consult a licensed professional before attempting any techniques outlined in this book. By reading this document, the reader agrees that under no circumstances is the author responsible for any losses, direct or indirect, that are incurred as a result of the use of the information contained within this document, including, but not limited to, errors, omissions, or inaccuracies.

# TABLE OF CONTENTS

**INTRODUCTION** — 8
- Why do you want to grow tea?
- Book Outline

**CHAPTER 1** — 12
**HISTORICI-TEA**
- What is Tea?
- What isn't tea?
- What are the most common tea types?
- Infusions
- Common Caffeinated Herbal Infusion Trees
- Common Caffeinated Fruits used for Fruit Infusions
- Common Non-Caffeinated Herbal & Fruit Infusion Ingredients

**CHAPTER 2** — 26
**QUALI-TEA**
- Tea Processing Techniques
- Leaf Size
- Tea Flush
- Cultivar
- Region

**CHAPTER 3** — 58
**AROUND THE WORLD IN EIGH-TEA DAYS**
- North America: 7 of the Most Common Teas & Herbal Infusions
- South America: 7 of the Most Common Teas, Herbal & Fruit Infusions
- Asia: 13 of the Most Famous Teas
- 3 Traditional Drinks & Inventions from Asia
- 3 Famous Fruit & Herbal Infusions from Asia
- Africa: 11 of The Most Common Teas & Infusions
- Europe: 8 Teas & Blends Common to Europe
- Oceania: 6 of the Most Common Teas, Blends & Infusions

**CHAPTER 4** — 93
**HOW TO GROW YOUR OWN TEA**
- The Basic Ideal Growing Conditions
- Finding the Right Location
- Methods of Planting
- Maintaining and Pruning
- Growing Tea in Any Climate

## CHAPTER 5          123
### HARVESTING & PROCESSING

Harvesting Basics
Ways to Harvest
White Tea & Yellow Tea
Green Tea
Oolong Tea
Black Tea
Dark Tea
Decaffeinating Tea
Storing Your Tea

## CHAPTER 7          159
### FORTY TEA RECIPES

Hot & Spiced Teas
Iced Teas
Tea Blends
Food Recipes with Tea

## CHAPTER 6          142
### PESTS, DISEASE & CULTIVATION

Pest Management
Tea Diseases
Cultivation

## FINAL REMARKS          200

## REFERENCES          202

## A Free Gift to My Readers!

<u>Don't just grow Tea, grow Vegetables & Herbs too!</u>

You may not be aware of the world of self-sufficiency which involves moving toward independence by removing our over reliance on the grid & systems we have created for everything our lives. Although you may not be looking to grow your own tea to be self-sufficient, it is a step in that direction.

I have a freebie for you to receive if you are interested. I'd also recommend my other book; Run from Easy which goes into detail about getting started in self-sufficiency if the topic is of interest to you.

Download My Free Self Sufficiency Planner At:
vaughanpublishing.activehosted.com/f/1
or scan the QR code.

This planner is designed to help you track your self-sufficiency journey in a practical financial way to see how much of your life is self-sufficient & generating income. This is completely free.

# INTRODUCTION

There's a time for war, and a time for peace,
A time to live, and a time to cease.
A time to work hard, and a time for sleep,
There's time for a break... that's the time for tea.

Although many take for granted how accessible it is to us, tea has become a big part of our modern lives. In so many cultures it is used to spend time with friends & family and as break from work a.k.a 'a tea break'. It's used in ceremonies and traditions all over the world, as gifts to diplomats and as a tool of hospitality when welcoming a stranger into one's home. Being the second most popular beverage in the world after water, the tea market is incredibly large, reeling in $7.44 Billion (£5.6 Billion) in 2019 [1]. Tea has a wide range of uses and prices. You can buy it in many forms, from tea bags to powdered forms as well as in loose tea leaf form. The price range within the tea market is very broad from the mass supermarket brands to the speciality tea brands. Although it is possible to buy very cheap tea bags, you usually get what you pay for.

My guess, is that **you**, having picked up this book, appreciate a good cuppa. You may not be a tea connoisseur, but you definitely enjoy a good quality

# INTRODUCTION

cup of tea and would generally opt for that over the very cheap brand tea bags that have poor quality taste, aroma & depth.

<u>The move toward self-sufficiency</u>: There has been a great crusade of people in recent days moving away from over dependence on consumerism as their means to live, starting afresh & becoming self-sufficient from the system, by growing their own vegetables, providing their own power, raising their own animals, collecting their own water, etc. Perhaps you find yourself in this self-sufficiency boat already and are looking to add tea growing to your repertoire. After all, if you currently spend a good penny on tea, growing & making your own tea may save you a few bob in the long run.

However, this may not be the case for everyone reading this. Some of you will just want to accept the challenge of growing something fresh for themselves, to see not only if you *can* do it, but if you can produce your own varieties & create tea recipes that are better than the shop bought brands.

Either way, it is always good to understand your 'why?' before embarking on any journey, and it is no different for the aspiring tea grower. Knowing your motivations for this passion project will help prevent you from being deterred by any hurdles you may face along the journey.

> ### Why do **you** want to grow tea?
>
> Tea growing in non-tropical climates is very much possible but isn't always successful. With this book as a guide, I hope you do find success and remain undeterred by the struggles you may face. Nevertheless, here are some of the common reasons for wanting to grow tea:
>
> 1. You want to be more self-sufficient: You may have already begun on the journey of self-sufficiency i.e., you've grown vegetables already, and this is the next step toward complete independence.
> 2. Perhaps you are an herb grower and think tea would partner well with the herbs you are already harvesting e.g., mint, lavender, etc. are very frequently used in infusions & tea recipes.
> 3. Perhaps you are an avid tea drinker looking for a new challenge and maybe hoping to cut down on you monthly tea bill.
> 4. Maybe you are an entrepreneur looking at starting your own speciality tea brand but have no idea how to get started.

Whatever your reason, this book is the right place to start. In this book, I will cover basic tea theory looking at what tea is and isn't, and the types of plants used for creating teas. Next, we will look at what makes quality tea, delving into the attributes of quality that can be determined prior to purchase. Following this I will travel the world with you and discuss the most common teas, tea blends & infusions across 7 continents, discussing their flavour profile, health benefits, and the sort of climates they grow in. Subsequently, with variety & theory in hand, I will go into detail about how to plant and grow your own tea at home! The section following this will detail how to maintain your tea plant through watering and pruning to make it grow into a thriving and fruitful tea bush. Once you've had success at this, you will find use of the chapters where I discuss the harvesting and processing of your tea leaves where you finally get to taste the fruit of your labours. We will look at the major tea types and how to harvest and process these at home with a mention on storing tea and making decaf tea. Following this, I will look at common tea plant pests and the deterrents to employ as well as looking at the tea diseases you may face and how you might treat them. The final section of the book is dedicated to recipes. There will be 4 sub sections including: hot & spiced teas to keep you warm in winter or whenever you fancy, iced teas to keep you cool in summer and enjoy in the garden or by the pool, tea blends you can try at home and finally tea food recipes to try with your harvested tea.

# Chapter 1
# HISTORICITEA

The first supposed mention of tea by an Englishman would be a letter from a Mr. Wickham, an employee of the East India Company written from Japan to Macau in China in 1615 where he mentions purchasing their best pot of "chaw", a word which sounds reasonably akin to the word "cha", meaning tea in Mandarin which is "ocha" in Japanese [33].

Most people agree that Japan and China have been using tea for thousands of years and that the tea plant is native to both nations. However, it's earliest use can be traced back to China, in 2737 B.C. where it was used by the Chinese emperor Shen Nung. Its earliest common use in society in China can be traced back to the Zhou Dynasty between 1100 B.C. and 771 B.C. where it was used for medicinal purposes [32].

Although many nations now have a history behind how this drink diffused its way into their respective society and culture, both China's & Japan's tea culture & history is very rich. Chinese tea culture, as we know it today, is given credit to the period known as the Tang Dynasty between 618 - 906 A.D., often referred to as the golden age of Chinese culture and art [32].

# CHAPTER 1: HISTORICITEA

From its health benefits to its medicinal properties, from its use in spiritual activity and use in social connection, the 10 main functions of tea drinking in China can be summarised below:

1. Drinking tea is considered beneficial for relieving fatigue, headaches as well as clearing one's body channels.
2. To be used as a hangover cure to dispel the effects of alcohol,
3. To remove hunger when combined with sauces in a porridge form,
4. To reduce the summer heat,
5. To lessen drowsiness,
6. To purify one's spirit and reduce anxiety,
7. To aid in the digestion of food,
8. To remove toxins from the body,
9. Drinking tea regularly is associated with long life,
10. Finally, tea drinking with the purpose to "invigorate the body" and "inspire the mind" [32].

As misleading as this chapter's title is, this book is not to be a history book that shows how tea has been intimately involved in shaping culture, politics, and social life throughout the last two thousand years. Neither is it about analysing the **historicity** of the evidence we have on tea's origin story. Rather, I wish for it to be a practical guide on how to grow tea at home. However, there are a few things that need to be covered first. Initially, I would like to cover the basics of tea theory. I promise, this will be both interesting and useful!

## What is tea?

I don't want to beat around the bush as it were. I would instead like to dive into what exactly, this bush is. To start, I do need to identify where the bounds of tea start and end and where they do not reach.

Tea has had a false representation in mainstream culture as a whole. Tea is often represented as any plant matter mixed with water, from flowers, to roots, to leaves. Some define it more strictly as a hot or cold beverage made from plant leaves with water, and some again would refine their definition even further to being a hot or cold beverage made with the caffeinated leaves of trees or plants. <u>All of these are wrong</u>.

Tea is defined as the beverages created solely from the plant species Camellia Sinensis [9]. Whether this is the Camellia Sinensis Var. Sinensis, the Camellia Sinensis Var. Assamica or the other two lesser-known variants, it must be made from this plant to qualify as being tea. Any other plant, tree or shrub that claims to be tea, is a wolf in tea's clothing.

## What isn't tea?

Many companies have created what they label as tea on the packet but is in fact made from caffeinated berries & other species of caffeinated plant. What is commonly called 'fruit tea' is more accurately defined as a fruit infusion. Similarly, what is commonly known as 'herbal tea' is more accurately defined as an herbal infusion. Nothing other than the 4 varieties of Camellia sinensis are officially classified as tea. Fruit infusions consist of a mixture of berries and plant matter and herbal infusions might be a mixture of leaves and flowers with some fruity addition. Some of these mainstream infusions do have caffeine in them but, many do not. If these herbs or fruits are mixed with tea leaves from the tea plant, then it can be classified as a tea or tea blend.

## What are the most common tea types?

If you are new to the world of tea, it may have surprised you to find out that almost every tea comes from the one plant. There are 6 main types of tea produced from this one plant. The main differences between them are to do with which part of the plant is harvested and used, the length of fermentation time applied to the leaves, as well as the specific processing techniques used to make the tea. Within these 6 main types, there exists a huge number of variations which are based on many different factors including:

<u>Where the tea is grown</u>
This encompasses the climate, the height above sea level, the soil quality and nutrients and the weather patterns, etc.

<u>When the tea is harvested</u>
The tea plant blossoms 3 or 4 times throughout the year. Depending on when it is harvested will change the shade, wetness & potency of the leaf. This will ultimately affect the flavour profile of the final tea.

<u>Which cultivar of tea you are using</u>
While there are four main variants of camellia sinensis, 1000's of cultivars exist. Each cultivar is slightly different with differences in leaf size and colour, root strength and length, the height it grows to, resistance to pests, adverse weather & disease, the balance of biochemicals in the leaf affecting flavour, caffeine content, & aroma, etc. More on this later.

<u>Processing technique & Post processing operations</u>
Most teas have some level of fermentation. The level to which this is done will change the flavour dramatically. The fermentation process is called oxidation. It is where the tea leaves are left to react with the air and turn a darker and darker brown colour. This has a major part to play in flavour. The level of fermentation is the main way to differentiate between the 6 major types of tea.

Any other additives employed during the tea post-processing will affect flavour as well. The leaf size produced by the type of tea production technique can affect the taste, quality, & price too.

Other factors that affect the quality of the final brew will be metrics like the quality of water used <u>in the brew</u>, specifically metrics like pH, Hardness & Ion Content etc [34]. Purifying the water often produces a better tasting tea than unprocessed chlorinated water [34]. However, factors like these are to do with the quality of the final brew taste rather than anything to do with the variation of tea itself.

The factors listed above are just an idea of the number of variations that can be created by changing one or more of these different parameters. In the next chapter we will delve deeper into the 6 main ways to differentiate tea based on quality mentioned above. For now, let's look at the major 6 types of tea, ordered according to their fermentation or oxidation period (least to most):

<u>White tea</u>

White tea is made from immature leaves and unopened buds. White teas typically have minimal processing; they are usually just dried, however some white teas are steamed and dried too [28].

### *Yellow tea*

This miracle tea is processed similar to green tea but with an additional step. The young leaves (somewhere between maturity and immaturity) are harvested, withered, rolled, and dried to prevent oxidation. Whilst undergoing the drying process, the leaves are encased and steamed [29]. An additional step called 'sealing yellow' is a smothering step which involves multiple cycles of slow roasting the tea leaves then a 24-hour cloth/paper drying process. This slow drying process removes the grassy taste of green tea [29].

### *Green tea*

Green tea is prepared from more mature leaves than white tea. Some of the leaves may even be withered. They are then steamed or fried, then rolled, and finally dried and post processed [28].

### *Oolong tea*

Tea leaves are "bruised" in order to increase oxidation however, they do not undergo full fermentation (oxidation). They are then heated and dried [28]. Oolong is translated in English as 'black dragon' and is also often referred to as 'blue tea' or 'blue green' tea.

### Black tea

Referred to as *Red Tea* in the east, Black Tea is probably the most popular of all the teas world-wide, drunk by millions every day. To make black tea, the leaves are fully rolled to maximise oxidation & are allowed to oxidise completely before drying, hence their dark brown colour [28].

### Dark tea

Referred to as *Black tea* in the East, this tea is often made from the Assamica variety. The leaves are heated and dried, then dampened before being pan-fired and compressed, very similar to black (*or red*) tea. It is then stored in a controlled environment and left to oxidise and ferment for decades. Pu-erh is one type of dark tea and is one of the most well-known. Some versions of ripened Pu-erh tea use a fungus called "Aspergillus Niger" to speed up this ageing process [28].

In Chapter 5, I will discuss in more practical detail how you can process each of the 6 types of tea at home.

## INFUSIONS

I will not refer to such beverages as herbal teas or fruit teas in this book, but as herbal/fruit infusions, to avoid confusion based on the definitions discussed earlier. Below, I address infusions in a bit more detail.

## Common Caffeinated Herbal Infusion Trees

Holly is a flowering plant species that can exist as a tree, a shrub or a plant and has over 600 species. Although many are used in herbal infusions, only 4 of these 600 officially contain caffeine:

1. Ilex Guayusa

More commonly known as Guayusa, this is an evergreen tree native to the Amazon Rainforest in South America, specifically the northern region that lies in Ecuador. Its leaves have revealed high antioxidant capacity, but this decreases with oxidation [35]. The leaves of this tree are used in a caffeinated herbal infusion named after the plant.

2. Ilex Cassine

Known as the Dahoon Holly or Cassena, this is grown in the states such as Virginia and Texas in the US, but also as far south as Mexico. This evergreen tree is also grown in Puerto Rico and the Bahamas as well.

### 3. Ilex Paraguariensis

Also known as Yerba mate, this holly shrub, which, at maturity, becomes a tree, is used in the production of the drink known as Mate, which is in the top 10 most popular caffeinated herbal infusions in the world.

### 4. Ilex Vomitoria

This is commonly known as the Yaupon Holly and its leaves were traditionally used by Native Americans to create caffeinated infusions. This is the second of the caffeinated hollies native to North America.

### *Ilex Tarapotina*

This species of Holly is rumoured to be the legendary fifth Holly shrub to have caffeine content in its leaves, although this is unofficial. This elusive species is native to Northern Peru and there is not much information about it yet. It is supposedly used to make a special type of mate known as "té o' maté".

## Caffeinated Fruits used in Fruit infusions

There are 5 main caffeinated seeds, beans, & cherries harvested from the fruits of fruit trees that are used in fruity infusions listed below:

| The Coffee Bean |
|---|

| The Kona Cherry |
|---|

| The Cocoa Bean |
|---|

| The Kola Nut |
|---|

| The Guarana Seed |
|---|

## Common Non-Caffeinated Herbal & Fruit Fusion ingredients

**Chamomile**: this herb's daisy-like flowers are regularly used in herbal infusions.

**Mint** (including peppermint & spearmint): another common household herb used in a variety of teas and infusions.

**Lemon:** Often used in conjunction with other ingredients in infusions e.g., Lemon & Ginger infusion, or Lemon & Green Tea. Also, one of the easiest drinks to make, lemon water; a drink that features in most kitchens and restaurants, would also count as a fruit infusion. Lemon is also used in many iced teas due to its refreshing, citrusy flavour.

**Rose:** The petals of this well-known flower often find their way not only into infusions but cordials, soaps, fragrances, and non-alcoholic mixers.

**Lavender:** Used in soaps, herbal infusions, and perfumes. It is particularly good to plant this near vegetables as it keeps away certain pests such as mosquitos, flies, moths, and fleas.

**Valerian:** Some claim this flower is the most effective natural sedative out there. Although the root is used in medicine, the human effects of the leaves are less well documented. The root, which can be bought in pre-portioned bags, can be brewed into an infusion.

**Ginger:** Another common household root. Can be used in dried or fresh form in infusions and in combination with other ingredients.

**Blood Orange:** The various health benefits of blood orange such as its antioxidant capabilities and cholesterol regulation properties make it a worthy inclusion to your fruit infusion cupboard [10].

**Strawberry**: The strawberry plant is what is a known as a Hardy plant. Hardy plants can resist unfavourable weather, such as frost, drought & cold winds, enabling the plant to survive year on year.

**Pineapple**: Pineapples are easy to grow in that all you require is the stalk from another pineapple to get going. Pineapple features in many perfumes and if you're in that camp... on pizza too.

**Raspberry**: a very useful fruit for making jams & preserves, for use in squashes & cordials and all manner of drinks including fruit infusions. Just as many make lemon water regularly for its health benefits, lemon & raspberry water is another common fruity infusion; just add water! Raspberry also often features in many iced teas.

**Nettle**: A really good use for this pesky weed is to stick its leaves in a mug with some boiling water and let it sit. You will be able to benefit from its anti-inflammatory effects as well as receiving an overall health boost to your kidneys, immune system, and digestion [11].

**Blueberry**: you can enjoy a nice warm blueberry infusion with a blueberry muffin if you'd like. Just don't confuse it with its alcoholic cousin; the blueberry tea cocktail, which has no blueberries or tea in it, but does have a bit of a kick.

As you can see, as soon as you delve into the world of non-caffeinated herbal or fruit infusion plants & trees, the list more or less extends to almost any plant, flower, root or fruit out there!

Beyond the list on the previous page, there is no limit to how you can combine parts of plants and fruits to create all kinds of infusions and creations. If you don't strictly have a definition for tea, then anything from a

# CHAPTER 1: HISTORICITEA

plant, mixed with hot or cold water becomes tea. Don't get me wrong, you can absolutely use everything from flowers, to plant roots, to berries to create these infusions, however, they are not tea by the strictest definition.

Furthermore, these non-caffeinated flowers, roots, plants & leaves can always be combined with traditional caffeinated tea (from the camellia sinensis plant) to create an unlimited number of variations in flavoured tea or tea blends e.g., Black Tea with Sicilian Orange or Green Tea with Mint.

Now you should have an apt understanding of how to categorise herbal infusions, fruit infusions as well as tea. While I implied that the Holly plant is the main contender in producing caffeinated herbal infusions, there are many non-caffeinated herbal infusions that are often thought to be tea, when they are not. In fact, the most famous misconception has yet to be unveiled, this is the South African herbal infusion known as Red Bush, also known as Rooibos. Although it features in many of your cupboards, it has been deceiving you if you thought it was tea.

From here on in the book though, I will be focusing mostly on tea, however Rooibos does make its return in Chapter 3 for you red bush fans out there.

# Chapter 2
# QUALI-TEA

There are 6 main ways to attribute quality to a specific tea other than the big two which are Aroma & Taste. The six other ways one could consider, are those you can determine prior to purchasing the tea. The six include the **Production Process**, the **Leaf size**, the **Tea Grade**, Which **Flush** it was harvested in, the **Cultivar** grown, & the **Region** it was grown in. In general terms, the most premium teas in the world come in the form of whole leaf teas, however that is not an accurate metric (alone) by which to measure two teas against each other; many broken or powdered teas may be of higher quality than their whole leaf contender. Hence, we need the other 5 indicators. While I could go into detail about each type of tea's grades & processing techniques, I will only briefly cover the most popular teas: black & green in this chapter. This is because in Chapter 5 we will be covering the home processing of each of the tea types in sufficient detail.

## TEA PROCESSING

### Black Tea Production Techniques

We have discussed the 6 types of tea that exist, however, within each type of tea, there are different manufacturing techniques used and within each of

# CHAPTER 2: QUALI-TEA

technique, there are distinctions & grades that attribute quality, flavour and of course, the final cost to the customer's wallet. Black tea has three main processing techniques.

1. Orthodox tea refers to the standard 5 step process used in black tea production. The 5 steps include withering, rolling, fermentation, drying and sorting. There are four leaf sizes that orthodox black tea production can produce: Whole leaf, Broken leaf, Fannings, and Dust.
2. CTC is another process used in black tea production. It is only a 3-step tea processing method: Crushing, Tearing & Curling. There are only three leaf sizes that CTC can produce: Broken Leaf, Fannings, and Dust.
3. There is a third method known as LTP which uses the Lawrie Tea Processor, but this is beyond the scope of this book.

Green Tea Production Techniques

There is one general processing method for green tea which comprises of withering, frying/steaming, drying, rolling, final drying, final rolling, & shaping. Some producers may vary the number of cycles of drying and rolling, others may have further post processes such as grinding into a powder or the use of frying instead of steaming for example. But the standard green tea process is as stated.

## Alternative Processing Techniques that give Attributed Quality

### Organic Tea

In general, anything organic has added value as it involves less chemicals and machine processing. It typically has more manual labour associated with it. In tea terms, this means that the soil is less subject to harmful chemicals associated with pests, and is less acidified, as only organic fertilisers are being employed. Also, the tea leaves are hand-picked and mostly hand processed. The factors that affect the direct treating of the plants and soil will have a more direct impact on quality & flavour of the tea leaves. Skilled hand processing also involves more care and gives more control over the consistency and flavours released. The added value, as well as its associated cost to implement, contribute to the higher price tag associated with organic tea.

### Panda Dung Tea

This tea is an example of a peculiar post processing technique which 'adds value'. As the name suggest, this tea is fermented in Panda Dung. The first batches in a year can cost up to $3,500 per 50 grams. The creator claims that because pandas do not absorb 70% of the food they consume, their faeces are high in nutrients. A nutty, mature taste is promised to those who would be willing to bite the bullet on the price tag and brave a sip of this strange tea. Its hefty price tag is supposedly more due to the rarity of the pandas rather than flavour profile it boasts.

## LEAF SIZE

The leaf size of a particular tea will correspond to how the final product is sold and brewed by the end consumer. It determines whether you will be brewing a spoonful of whole tea leaves in your teapot or if you are using a tea bag in your mug which commonly sits in the 'broken leaf' grouping, or if you are using tea shingles which is a coarse powder (Fannings) or, finally a fine tea powder (Dust).

## TEA GRADES

### Black Tea Grades

Within each tea production technique, and within each type of leaf size, there exists many different tea grades which indicate the quality of the leaves used from the specific tea plant that was harvested. It is hard to come up with a concise and consistent list of tea grades because each country and plantation appears to have their own standard for their tea. I have tried to list some of the most common black and green tea grades as listed by the Indian Tea Association in the following pages. Another problem is that one plantation might elevate the standard of their tea to a higher rank when, in another country,

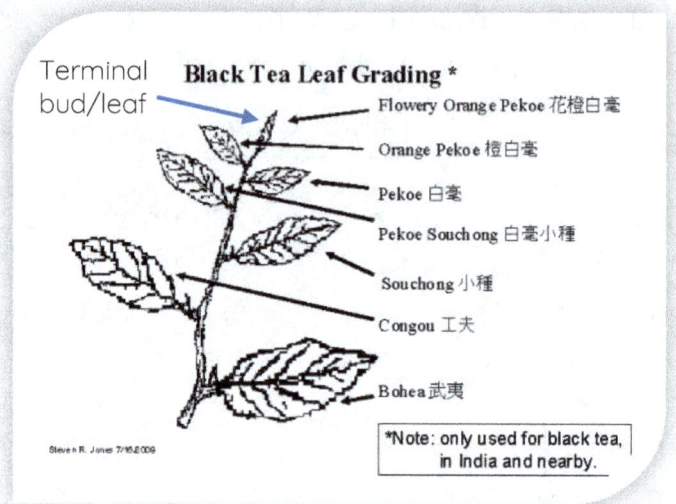

this could be considered average. What I mean by this is, the orange pekoe in China may be very different to the orange pekoe produced in Russia for example. This makes it very tricky and confusing to know, purely based on production technique, leaf size and tea grade, if the tea is of high quality or not. However, what the tea grades do tell us, is which leaves are used from the tea plant, which is usually an indication of the quality specific to that tea plant and that tea plantation. Orange Pekoe and Flowery Orange Pekoe use the best leaves on the tea plant. On the black tea leaf grading image above, attributed to reference [74], you can see an example of which leaves are used to produce which types of tea. The ones nearer the top are used in higher quality teas.

Below I have listed the main black tea grades for Orthodox & CTC Black Tea Production Methods [73]:

| Orthodox Whole Leaf Black Tea | | |
|---|---|---|
| Grade | Nomenclature | Description |
| Bohea | As stated. | Uses the leaves as indicated by the picture on previous. Lower down leaves indicate lower quality tea. |
| Congou | As stated. | Sometimes combined with other plants during processing e.g., Rose Congou tea. |
| S | Souchong | Used in Lapsang Souchong, a very popular black tea. |
| P | Pekoe or PS (Pekoe Souchong) | Shorter and smaller leaves using the leaves indicated by the picture above. |
| OP | Orange Pekoe | Long wiry leaf without tips and has a light liquor |
| FOP | Flowery Orange Pekoe | Long leaf and few tips |
| GFOP | Golden Flowery Orange Pekoe | Higher proportion of tips. The leaves & buds have a golden tint. |
| TGFOP | Tippy Golden Flowery Orange Pekoe | Highest proportion of tips with golden tips & leaves. |
| FTGFOP | Finest Tippy Golden Flowery Orange Pekoe | Nicknamed 'Far Too Good For Ordinary People', such teas are from some of the finest regions in the world. |
| SFTGFOP | Special Finest Tippy Golden Flowery Orange Pekoe | Only the highest quality and most premium teas are reserved for this category. |
| **Orthodox Broken Black Tea** | | |
| BPS | Broken Pekoe Souchong | Medium sized knobby like tea |

| | | |
|---|---|---|
| BOP | Broken Orange Pekoe | Medium sized with tip ends |
| GBOP | Golden Broken Orange Pekoe | Medium sized with tip ends and golden tinge |
| FBOP | Flowery Broken Orange Pekoe | Medium sized with more tip ends |
| GFBOP | Golden Flowery Broken Orange Pekoe | Medium sized with more tip ends and golden tinge |
| TGFBOP | Tippy Golden Flowery Broken Orange Pekoe | Made from the Top-Quality leaves with a high proportion of golden tips. From Darjeeling & a few areas in Assam. |
| **Orthodox Fannings Black Tea** | | |
| PF | Pekoe Fannings | As described above but ground finer. |
| OF | Orange Fannings | Medium even sized coarse powder |
| FOF | Flowery Orange Fannings | Medium even sized coarse powder with tips |
| GFOF | Golden Flowery Orange Fannings | Medium even sized coarse powder with tips. Some or all leaves & tips used may have a golden tinge. |
| TGFOF | Tippy Golden Flowery Orange Fannings | As described above but with more tips. |
| BOPF | Broken Orange Pekoe Fannings | As described above but ground into finer. |
| **Orthodox Dust Black Tea** | | |
| OD | Orthodox Dust | Made using lower grade leaves |
| OPD | Orthodox Pekoe Dust | As described above but ground finer. |
| OCD | Orthodox Churamani Dust | Clean black tea |
| BOPD | Broken Orange Pekoe Dust | As described in BOP but ground finer. |

# CHAPTER 2: QUALI-TEA

| BOPFD | Broken Orange Pekoe Fine Dust | As described in BOPD but ground even finer. |
|---|---|---|
| FD | Fine Dust | |
| D-A | Dust Grade A | |
| GD | Golden Dust | |
| SPL. D | Special Dust | |

There are other grades that exist between these grades which aren't listed e.g., SFTGFOP1, OP(A): Orange Pekoe Grade A, or BOP1: Broken Orange Pekoe Grade 1, etc. Below, I have listed the main CTC grades based on the 3-leaf sizes produced.

| CTC Broken Leaf Black Tea ||
|---|---|
| **Grade** | **Name** |
| FP | Flowery Pekoe |
| BPS | Broken Pekoe Souchong |
| PEKOE | Pekoe |
| BOP (L/ /sm) | Broken Orange Pekoe (Large/Standard/Small) |
| BP (/sm) | Broken Pekoe (Standard /Small) |
| CTC Fanning Leaf Black Tea ||
| OF | Orange Fannings |
| PF | Pekoe Fannings |
| BOPF | Broken Orange Pekoe Fannings |
| CTC Dust Leaf Black Tea ||
| PD | Pekoe Dust |
| D | Dust |
| CD | Churamani Dust |
| GD | Golden Dust |
| SRD | Super Red Dust |
| FD | Fine Dust |
| SFD | Super Fine Dust |

## Green Tea Grades

There are too many inconsistent systems that exist to measure and grade green tea, making it difficult to measure teas from different countries against each other. There is an Indian system, a Chinese system, a

Taiwanese system and a Japanese system for grading green tea. Some countries such as Korea, merely categorise their green tea based on the flush alone (detailed in the next section). Many Japanese green teas are in powdered form such as Matcha, so grading based on leaf size is of little use. Nevertheless, as it is impossible for me to detail all the different grading systems without this book becoming a tea encyclopaedia, I have only listed a few of the grades again detailed by Indian Tea Association, with one or two additions [73].

| \multicolumn{3}{c}{Whole Leaf Green Tea} | | |
|---|---|---|
| Grade | Name | Description |
| TWANKY | Twanky green tea | Uses old ragged opened leaves, an inferior green tea. |
| YH | Young Hyson (Lucky Dragon Tea) | Long and twisted leaves, but thinly rolled, that will unfurl when brewed |
| FYH | Fine Young Hyson | A refined version of YH |
| **Broken Leaf Green Tea** | | |
| GP | Gun Powder | Withered, fired and rolled into balls or 'bullets' which unfurl when brewed |
| H | Hyson | Broken version of hyson |
| FH | Fine Hyson | Broken version of FYH |
| **Fannings Green Tea** | | |
| SOUMEE | Soumee | Using 1-1.5mm sized leaves, Soumee is only one type of Fannings green tea |
| **Dust Green Tea** | | |
| DUST | Dust | Green Tea Dust |

CHAPTER 2: QUALI-TEA

## TEA FLUSHES

A flush refers to the new growth of leaves from a period of dormancy which instigates a new harvesting period. There are 3 or 4 main flushes a tea plant undergoes in a year and 2 additional minor ones in India. However, the number of flushes and times the tea plant can be harvested per year is heavily weather dependant. Tea harvested from the first flush or first quality harvest for that region is generally more expensive but does not necessarily indicate the quality of taste, as each flush will give unique flavours and characteristics to the tea leaves.

- **First Flush** [65]**: March – April:** It typically represents the start of spring. The most premium teas are attributed to this harvesting season as the tea plants have rested during the winter and rejuvenated their nutrients from the soil. The more premium harvesters might reserve a section of their plantation to only be harvested once a year during the first flush. The highest yield is also in the first flush usually. To visualise this, if a tea field produces 8000 kg of tea leaves in the first harvest, the second harvest might yield around 6000 kg, and 4000 kg in the third harvest [66].
This first harvest season is referred to as Ichibancha in Japan.

- **Second Flush [65]: May – June:** This harvest season is referred to as <u>Nibancha</u> in Japan & represents the late spring to mid-summer time. Many high-quality teas come from this harvesting season. Generally, depending on the region, the 1st or 2nd flush teas are the highest qualities in flavour with every other flush being inferior. For example, the 2nd flush in Assam in India has won many awards whereas the higher quality tea in Darjeeling in India, is the 1st flush. However, it is unlikely a 3rd flush will ever produce higher quality than the 1st or 2nd.
- **Monsoon Flush (Third) [65]: July- September:** This third flush is called the monsoon flush due to the large number of monsoons that occur in India in this time of year, though, it isn't labelled as this in non-tropical locations. Depending on where you are in the world, and whether you get heavy rain during this period, will determine what your third flush delivers. Generally, anything after the 1st and 2nd flush tends not to be used in premium tea. However, in India, tea harvested during the monsoon flush is used in the popular sweet beverage, Masala Chai. This flush is typically mid-summer to Autumn time and in Japan, this harvest season is referred to as <u>Sanbancha</u>.

- **Autumn Flush (Fourth) [65]: October- mid December:** This harvest season is referred to as Yonbancha in Japan. Not many countries will have the climate that allows a fourth yield during this time.

Tea plants often remain dormant from mid-December to end of February *or* whenever the winter season occurs in that region. This is when the plant recovers, rejuvenates, and reabsorbs its much-needed nutrients. This is not the case for countries with no winter or mild winter climates, for example, tropical rainforest countries. In such places, although their tea can be harvested year-round, the plantations will use harvesting strategies to allow the plants to rest and recover so they are ready for their quality harvesting seasons.

The first two flush periods of early spring to mid-summer are as close to being universal across all the world as you will get but will still differ on the exact months they occur and frequency of harvesting. Although a monsoon season may only occur in some countries, you may still be able to harvest until mid-autumn time, again weather dependant. There are differences in the harvesting strategies depending on region, country, and individual plantation. As general rule, in a peak season, tea is harvested every 7-10 days whereas, in a 2nd and 3rd flush, the harvesting frequency may lower to every 2 weeks.

**Tropical Climates:** Sri-Lankan (Ceylon) tea can be harvested all year round due to the steady tropical climate there. However, as any plant needs time to rest, there are two main quality harvesting seasons employed in Sri-Lanka. In Nuwara Eliya for example, these two quality seasons will be 1st from January to March, which is earlier than China and Japan, and the 2nd flush being from July to September. Other tropical locations where tea can be harvested all year round are places such as Nilgiri (India) & Kenya, etc, but again, harvesting strategies are applied. The business ramifications of when tea is harvested in that plantation need to be considered too, for example, harvesting & processing the tea so it is ready to be sold when the demand for tea is high, but supply is low.

**China harvesting:** China has different times for harvesting their tea based on the festivals in their Lunisolar Calendar [67][70]. Typically, these harvesting periods are followed mainly for their finer and high-quality teas so will involve the harvesting of the best leaves and buds. For example, their first flush, called Ming Qian, will typically involve harvesting in March up until the 4th - 6th April when the Qingming festival usually falls. After this they have a few other harvesting periods in close succession such as Yu Qian from around the 6th of April to April 20th, then the third flush is Gu Yu from around the 21st of April to May 6th [67][70]. Finally, you have Li Xia which is the fourth harvesting season from May 7th to May 21st [67][70]. As I stated before, this is usually for the best leaves and buds. The lower leaves used in other less premium teas and blends may be harvested up until November time. Dan Cong is an exception which is a rare tea grown in the Phoenix Mountains. This can be harvested in late Autumn/Winter months toward December time.

I have created a rough timeline on the next page showing the flushes and their associated countries based on various resources: see references [67][68][69][70][71][72]. On some of the countries I have indicated the harvesting frequency. This timeline is only a rough picture rather than an accurate or exact representation. My hope is that you would be able to refer to this yourself when you come to harvesting and, wherever you are in the world, match your micro-climate to one of these major tea harvesting countries. Then you will be able to gauge approximately when you can or should be harvesting your tea.

# TEA-MING WITH LIFE

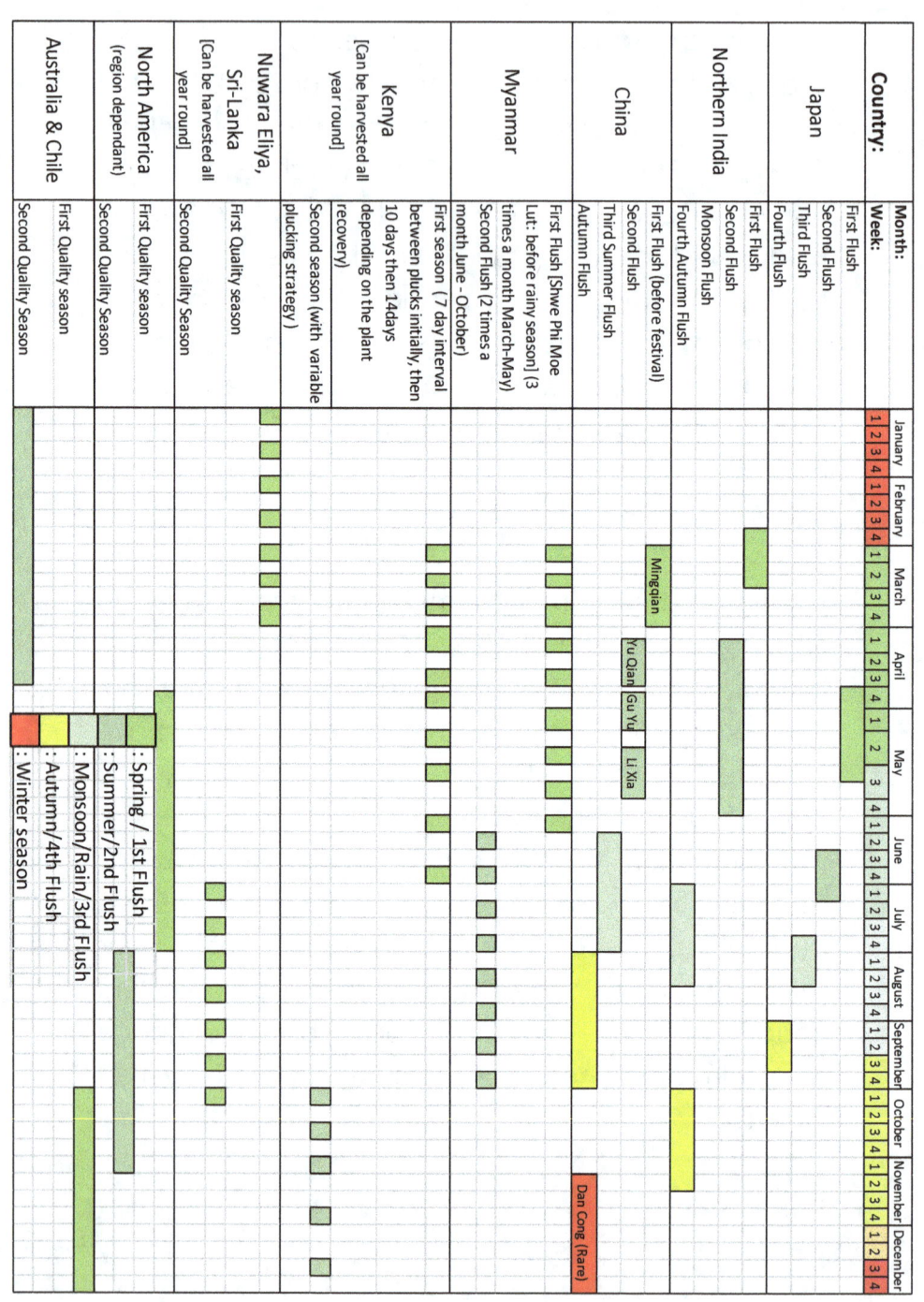

40

## Summarising Tea Quality Based On Tea Flushes.

The easiest way to know if you are getting the best quality from a specific plantation is to find out if the tea is from the first or second flush. If it is from their late summer to Autumn harvest (3$^{rd}$ flush) or later, it is unlikely to be the best quality tea that plantation can offer.

One other factor I haven't mentioned is that the exact time of the plant's flushes will vary slightly depending on which cultivar is grown. We will look at cultivars in the next section but details on which cultivar blooms when, is beyond the scope of this book.

## Relevance To Growing Your Own Tea

From the perspective of one looking to grow their own tea, if your country experiences four distinct seasons, it will be much easier for you to figure out when to harvest your tea and when to prune it as opposed to those of you who live in extreme climates or wildly varying temperatures.

**In summary:**

- If you have four seasons, follow the general trend of Early Spring (1$^{st}$ flush), Early Summer (2$^{nd}$ flush), Late Summer (3$^{rd}$ Flush), Autumn (4th flush),

Winter (rest). The 3$^{rd}$ & 4$^{th}$ flushes aren't compulsory to harvest.
- If you live in a tropical location, i.e., ideal weather all year, you could attempt to adopt the practise of another nation of similar climate like Kenya or Sri-Lanka. For example, employing 2 or 3 major harvesting seasons with medium rests between harvests and one large rest at the end of the last harvest for that year.
- If you live in extreme climates, refer to the section about growing tea in any climate. In terms of when to harvest, you will have to create a unique harvesting strategy as your tea's environment is both controlled & artificial. In this case, you will need to wait for the first flush & use that as the period you harvest your first flush every year. Your 2$^{nd}$ flush would be 1.5 months later & again 1.5 months later for the 3$^{rd}$ and 4$^{th}$, should you decide to harvest these. After this, you would have a rest period of around 3-5 months until the same time next year when you notice the first new growth. However, I only recommend heavy harvesting strategies when your plant is strong and has undergone decentering pruning to make the bush low and wide with many new shoots ready to be harvested.

Now I will move on to the penultimate way to gauge the quality of a particular tea prior to purchasing it. This is the type of cultivar that is being grown.

## CULTIVARS

Thankfully, we don't have to rely only on the production process used, the leaf size or the tea grade to determine quality. We have 2 more ways to determine quality: The cultivar it comes from and the region/country it is grown in. While there are four main varieties of the tea plant, there are 1,500 cultivars that have been derived. A cultivar is an abbreviation for a **Culti**vated-**Var**iety, bred either naturally or intentional by humans to exhibit certain characteristics [73]. This is done by cross-pollinating plants, for example, a Chinese tea plant Camellia Sinensis var. Sinensis with an Indian tea plant Camellia Sinensis var. Assamica. The Camellia Sinensis var. Cambodiensis is a third variety that is hardly ever used in producing tea, however, is infrequently used in creating new cultivars [73].

You may, for example wish to take the height of plant-A and pair it with the fermentation ability of plant-B, or a tea plant that retains more antioxidants in the hot sun with one that rejuvenates it leaves quickly [73]. You can even cross pollinate non-tea plants with the tea plant to propagate certain characteristics. The possibilities of cultivation are pretty much endless. That being said, it is not a straightforward or simple process, and you are not guaranteed any desired results. I have made a section on this later in the book on how to do this at home without any fancy lab equipment. I don't intend to go into detail about all the different types of cultivars, but below, I've stated a few common ones.

> 1. Yabukita (Japan): This cultivar represents approximately 75% of Japanese tea production including green and black tea. Other cultivars used in Japan are Yutakamidori, Sayamakaori, Kanayamidori, & Okumidori [66].

2. Qing Xin (Taiwan): This small dense bush once accounted for 40% of Taiwan's tea production and was created by Taiwan's Tea Research Extension Stations (TRES) [75].

> 3. Jin Xuan (Taiwan): This higher yielding cultivar, produces teas with a "light, creamy flavour, and is often marketed as 'milk oolong'" [75].

4. Ruby #18 (Taiwan): This cultivar took almost 500 years to make and is a cross between an Assam tea plant and a wild Taiwanese plant. It is marginally sweet, with a fruity aroma and subtle notes of mint & spice.

> 5. Tie Guanyin (China): This is a premium Chinese cultivar. Tea from this cultivar is expensive. See the Asia grown teas section for more info [75].

CHAPTER 2: QUALI-TEA

6. Qi Dan (China): This cultivar is a rock growing plant which is used to make oolong tea. Teas from cuttings of this cultivar are the most expensive in the world [75]. See the Asia grown teas section for more info.

7. Long Jing #43 (China): One of the main cultivars used to make the popular green tea called Long Jing or Dragon Well tea and is grown in the west lake area [75]. See the Asia grown teas section for more info [75].

8. Zhu Ye Zhong (China): This is the cultivar most often used in the production of Chinese Keemun tea [75].

9. AV2 (India): produced using a process called vegetative propagation, this cultivar has been adopted by many farmers in Darjeeling [75]. As a result, much of recent Darjeeling tea comes from this cultivar.

10. TRFK 306/1 (Kenya): This cultivar has become famously known around the world as Purple Tea. It boasts, higher yields, greater resistance to unfavourable climate and higher antioxidants [40] [75]. See the Africa grown teas section for more info.

Creating cultivars is a controlled scientific process of changing the exact biochemicals in the tea leaves as well as the characteristics of the plant. This is why it can take so long to do. There are factors associated with cultivars that affect the plants longevity e.g., resistance to disease, adverse weather, etc, there are factors that affect plant yield e.g., regrowth time, root length, ability to grow in unfavourable climate, etc, finally there are factors affecting quality of the tea flavour e.g., biochemicals in the tea such as the chlorophyll content (associated with colour), the flavonoid & caffeine content (associated with the tea's flavour), etc. Plantations need to weigh up the pros and cons of cultivars to pick the best one for their climate and which will be more favourable to their business from a monetary point of view e.g., higher yield being more important than flavour if they are aiming to produce mass market tea bags. If you are growing tea with the end goal of making a business out of it, this is something you will need to consider as well. If you are growing speciality tea, higher quality of taste is of more importance. If you are growing tea only for only you and your family, then I would advise going for a higher quality tasting cultivar provided it can thrive in the weather specific to your location.

## Cultivars of Highest Quality

I wouldn't be able to give you an overview of important cultivar indicators without mentioning some scientific jargon. Before reading the below I want to remind the reader that green tea and black tea are at opposite ends of the spectrum with regards to oxidation. Green tea undergoes little oxidation and Black tea is fully oxidised.

It is agreed that important flavonoid biochemicals present in tea leaves such as catechins are good indicators for determining a tea's quality [25][77]. One study that measured the catechin content of different cultivars showed that the Assamica variety had the highest levels of catechins followed by Cambod, which is a cultivar made from an Assam tea plant & a Chinese tea plant [76]. This was followed by the Chinese tea plant variety [76]. However, the catechin content of the leaves prior to processing is not something that is usually detailed on the packet of tea when you buy it. Nor is there a complete database of the 1500 cultivars and their contents of each of these. At least not one I am aware of.

Although the catechin content of the leaf is a good indicator of quality and is influenced by the cultivar used, it is important to note that the catechin content is more greatly influenced by regional/locational factors [79], See next section.

Another study found that a higher ratio of amino acid to flavonoids is more desirable and is attributed to higher quality green teas [65]. A different study found that a ratio of flavonoids to amino acids of less than 8 is ideal for green tea, whereas a ratio of 15 or greater is ideal for black tea production [25]. It details for example, that albino cultivars, which are good for making green tea, have higher levels of amino acids and lower levels of catechins & caffeine [25]. Furthermore, a different report affirms that, it is the oxidation of these catechins that produces products such as theaflavins & thearubigins, giving rise to what we would call 'black tea quality attributes' [77]. Consequently, higher levels of catechins, <u>along with oxidation</u>, will increase these theaflavins & thearubigins products and, as a result, increase the **black** tea attributes associated with quality. The thearubigin biochemical controls the body (thickness), colour, & the taste of the black tea whereas the theaflavins control the briskness & brightness of the tea [90].

The findings from all these studies detailed above corroborate one another and so, in terms of cultivars, I would associate a higher amino acid to polyphenol/flavonoid ratio in a tea's leaves to a higher quality green tea. I would associate a higher polyphenol/flavonoid to amino acid ratio with a higher quality black tea once fully oxidised (catechins oxidise into the theaflavins and thearubigins).

*Pro Tip #1: The ideal ratio of theaflavins to thearubigins for a quality black tea is between 1:10 to 1:12 [90]. By increasing the fermentation time, this ratio increases.*

When buying tea from plantations, you may not be able to figure out on the packet the ratios of these biochemicals in the tea leaves. However, if you can find out the type of cultivar, you may be able to go away and research this online if the biochemical ratio exists online.

## A word on climate change

As climate change increases, certain characteristics of the problem such as increased $CO_2$ & temperature will benefit tea plants, whereas drought, less rainfall, etc. will affect it negatively [80]. Moving forward, new cultivars need to be bred to survive more extreme conditions i.e., deeper roots and higher amino acid & sugar content retention [80]. These cultivars will be of higher value than those which cannot survive droughts in the future. Additionally, cultivars bred to survive higher heats and those that have a high photosynthesis rate in response to rising $CO_2$ levels, could be a way of fighting climate change. How the propagating of these new cultivars will affect the final taste of the tea will require a lot of further research.

So.... How does this apply to you, the soon to be tea grower? Well, if you are in a part of the world that is currently being affected by climate change, I would advise researching the types of cultivars that are out there and investing in a cultivar that will thrive in the changing conditions suited to your microclimate. Then you will be future ready. For now, we will head on to the final section on quali-tea theory, Region.

# REGION

## Biggest importers and exporters of tea

The top 5 exporters of tea globally are China, India, and Kenya, followed by Sri-Lanka, and the United Arab Emirates (re-exporter). The greatest importers of tea are Pakistan, United states, Russia, Hong Kong, and the U.K. In this section we will look at regional factors influencing quality and in the next chapter, we will discuss the different teas & infusions from around the globe along with their origin which will hopefully whet your appetite to get started in producing your own tea.

## Regional Factors affecting Tea Quality

Prime Climate Conditions: Tropical conditions where there is plenty of rainfall and plenty of sunshine is ideal for the tea plant. Temperatures in the range of -20°C in the Himalayas through to 35°C in Kenya have allowed for tea survival. Depending on the cultivar though, its ideal temperature may vary. The most normal temperature range for growing tea is 13°C - 26°C (during spring and summer) and the most ideal temperature range for growth is 18°C - 23°C. This is further backed up by the section below that shows the change in yield with temperatures well outside of this range. Tea may survive in temperatures up to

40°C, but it may struggle to yield. When tea is exposed to temperatures of -10°C or lower for extended periods of time, the tea plant will likely get damaged.

Extreme weather affecting yields: Extreme weather in China affects the yields of the Camellia Sinensis. In a research paper studying the effects of the weather and tea yield in China, it was found that in extreme cold weather in China, the yield was reduced by a maximum of 56.3% [55]. They found that each day the tea crop was exposed to extreme cold (0°C - 4°C) the yield decreased around 2%-4% [55]. On the other end of the spectrum, each day the tea was exposed to extreme heat (34°C-36°C), the yield decreased by around 3.7% [55].

Soil pH: A research paper on the pH of soil in China for growing tea showed that the ideal pH for growing it is in the mildly acidic range of 4.5 to 5.5 [56], however it normally exists in the range 3.5 to 6.5 [80]. The normal range for soil moisture is 60-95% but the optimum is 70-90% moisture. This is in terms of percentage water retention [80].

Soil acidification is a big issue when you don't take enough care and over intensely abuse your agricultural systems. Only 43.9% of soil in China is estimated to be in the ideal range for growing tea whereas 46% of its soil has become too acidic (outside the ideal range) [56]. Chemical fertiliser application is clearly to blame for this as the organic tea plantations showed no substantial sign of soil acidification [56]. This is an important note for growing your own tea. Using chemical fertilisers and pesticides may damage your yield, plant, and soil in the long run. It is important to monitor the pH of the soil you use once or twice a year.

Soil moisture/texture: The tea plant generally does not take deep roots which makes it susceptible to flooding & drought. It is important not to have soil that is too dry or drains too quickly. Using thicker soil will do this, such as clay peat. Make sure it's not too thick if you have a high amount of rainfall, otherwise you will not have sufficient drainage and will flood the plant. The soil in your region may or may not be good for growing, you need to assess this and, if it isn't good (i.e., too dry or too thick), to purchase some new soil or treat or supplement the existing soil.

Soil Nutrients: Volcanic soil is rich in minerals and nutrients and tea grown in it often boasts unique flavours and a higher price tag.

Air Content: Very high elevations will reduce the amount of air density. Also, areas with high levels of $CO_2$ will make the tea thrive more.

Water Quality: the water quality fed to the tea plants is important as these carry new nutrients and minerals to restore the soil and feed the plants. Mountain streams & areas with naturally occurring salts will add further nutrients to the soil. Rainfall is also going to be better than chlorinated tap water as well. If you are on the road to becoming self-sufficient, rainwater harvesting is a way to do this. Alternatively, many people use their grey water to feed their garden to make their water go further. Some even reuse the water a second time by retrieving the water that drains through the soil & pump it back into their toilet to use again for flushing. If you do use grey water to feed plants, be careful what you use on the tea plant that it doesn't contain anything that could damage it such as soaps and chemicals. Mitigate this through filtration.

Elevation: A study that measured the effect of elevation on the polyphenol content and amino acid content in the tea leaves grown in 5 locations in China, showed that as the elevation increased from 212m up to 1020m, the tea from the plantations had less polyphenols (i.e., flavonoids such as catechins) and more amino acids [80]. Based on what was discussed in the cultivars section, this would make higher altitudes more favourable to quality green tea production. If you are in a country or region that is of higher altitude, your environment may be better suited to green tea. Whereas if you are based in a region that is closer to sea-level, quality black tea production may be more favourable. Bear in mind also that with the 6 tea types listed earlier in the book going down from white tea to dark tea, you increase in oxidation as you go down the list. This could apply to the teas which require more oxidation as well i.e., oolong, black & dark teas. This factor shouldn't be used in isolation and definitely should not deter you from trying to produce all 6 types if you can.

Light Conditions: Generally, areas with more solar radiation will experience higher yields but these can be optimised even more with diffused light if the right level of overcast weather is present [80]. Intense light means more heat and should be paired with moist soil of course. Jungle areas that grow tea, will have a natural light diffusion which is good for tea growth. Some teas are intentionally grown in the shade prior to harvesting to darken the leaves. Some harvesters grow intentional shade trees to further control lighting conditions.

## Regional Factors affecting Attributed Quality

Origin story: Teas with Interesting Origins, Myths, Legends, or Famous individuals who have drunk it, are all things that can help attribute quality to a particular tea brand but have no bearing on the quality of tea itself. This would be considered attributed quality or added value.

<u>Age of tree/cultivar</u>: This also adds the perceived value to the tea and can also directly affect the tea quality. It is also part of the tea's origin story.

## Regions of Highest Quality Teas

As you would expect, the places of highest quality tea are those with richest soil, long history in the art of tea processing, high elevation, and tropical climate. Some of the regions producing the highest quality teas are:

- India: Assam $2^{nd}$ flush tea and Darjeeling $1^{st}$ flush tea, both in India.
- Japan: Shizuoka, Kagoshima, & Uji regions in Japan,
- Ceylon: Nuwara Eliya, Dimbula, & Uda Pusellawa areas in Sri-Lanka,
- Taiwan: Ali Shan, Yu Shan, and Li Shan regions in Taiwan,
- China: Zhejiang, Fujian, Yunnan, and the Anhui provinces in China.

Of course, it's hard to come up with an absolutely perfect list for the highest quality tea regions in the world but these 5 countries are the most likely to win even if the regions within them are subject to change.

## Controlling Regional Factors

The main factors you can control are soil & water quality and pH. Lighting and temperature can be controlled a bit more using shade trees. If you are growing your tea bush in a large pot, you will be able to control the sunlight it receives by moving the pot. However, if you intend to use a pot or container for your tea's permanent home, then the size of pot should be quite large and would be quite impractical to move it around all the time. However, this is a feasible option if you have mild winters ideal for tea but extremely hot summers or vice versa. Finally, although you can't completely control heavy wind, rain & frost, you can provide rain cover, wind breakers and mulch to help mitigate the effects of these slightly.

> Another important note. Although you wouldn't be able to determine these prior to purchase, aroma & taste will always be the best indicators of quality. Reviews on products often give you a good indicator of what to expect so always start there when looking to buy your tea.

# CHAPTER 2: QUALI-TEA

### A Note to Those Starting a Tea Growing Business...

In less dense markets such as countries that produce very little tea, it may be easier to sell your tea as speciality or what is labelled as high quality, purely based on which leaves you are using, the flush, the grade, and the cultivar. The mere fact that tea grown in your country is rare will be a Unique Selling Point for you, and will be a draw or allure to many tea fanatics. Also, if your tea growing origin story is somewhat interesting, it is easy to make your tea seem rare, high-quality and speciality, even if its overall quality and flavour doesn't quite match up to the quality and flavour of premium teas out of India and China. Anyone looking to start growing their own tea in a country that produces very little tea, and wanting to commercialise it, take note...

## Chapter 3
## AROUND THE WORLD IN EIGH-TEA DAYS

As much as I'd like to say there were eighty teas in this section, alas I have misled you again. I just couldn't resist the chapter title. In all honesty, here are 58 teas, blends & infusions from across 7 continents.

### North America
### The 7 Most Common Teas & Herbal Infusions

1. **Green Tea**
2. **White Tea**
3. **Black Tea**
4. **Oolong Tea**

These 4 are the most common teas exported from the US. In America, tea plantations extend from the tropical island of Hawaii & South-eastern states along the coast to Canada, with a few scattered along the North Western states. While the US isn't a large exporter of tea, it is the $2^{nd}$ largest importer worldwide, with around 75% of its consumption being attributed to iced tea. The US tea growing market suffers from the fact that most of the US doesn't have a tropical climate as in the Asia or in South America. Also, speciality tea brands can struggle to compete with mass produced supermarket brands. On top of this, labour in the US costs more than in Asia & South America. Speciality Tea is often about where its grown, its origin, climate & history. Not many plantations in the US have that Unique Selling Point (USP), & so the number of successful ones is few.

### 3. Yaupon

As discussed prior, this is an herbal infusion made from the Yaupon Holly which is <u>native</u> to North America. It doesn't have the bitter taste associated with coffee due to its lack of tannin. This caffeinated plant certainly has that USP and some companies have capitalised on it.

### 4. Cassena

A close relative to the Yaupon, the Dahoon Holly also known as Cassena is a plant that is also native to the southeast coast of the US as well as Mexico, the Bahamas, Puerto Rico & Cuba.

### 5. Red Rose Herbal Infusion

A Canadian Rose Herbal Infusion Company, now called Red Rose, began trading back in 1894, over a 100 years ago and you guessed it, their beverages feature dried, non-caffeinated red rose petals [12].

## SOUTH AMERICA
## 7 Popular Teas, Herbal & Fruit Infusions

### 1. Colombian Black

Colombian black, green & white teas, both standard and organic are grown high up in the Andes mountains in volcanic soil that is rich in nutrients and minerals which creates these amazing rich tea flavours.

### 2. Yerba Mate

Yerba mate is a drink that is made using leaves from one of the four caffeinated holly trees and is consumed in a hollow gourd with a metal or wooden straw called a bomba (pictured). It can be drunk hot or iced with water, juice or milk and is typically consumed in social settings such as breakfast and as an alternative afternoon tea. Mate is one of the most popular herbal infusions globally with a market size of $189M in 2019 [1]. According to the Observatory of Economic Complexity, the largest exporters of Mate in 2019 were Argentina (44%) at $83.1M and Brazil (42.9%) at $81M and Paraguay (3.81 %) at $7.2M, with the largest importers being Uruguay (35.9%) and Syria (31.7%) and Chile (6.02%) at $11.4M [1]. With the exception of Syria's adoption of the beverage when immigrants fell in love with the drink and began exporting it to their motherland just before World War II, this drink's popularity is heavily localised to South America [8].

The tree is native to the Atlantic Forest in Brazil and unfortunately due to the growing demand for the product there has been a lot of deforestation caused by the increase in cattle ranching, soybean production & yerba mate harvesting [4]. Interestingly some companies such as Guayaki Yerba Mate have an ethical business model which is both generating profit and restoring the ecology and culture of the Atlantic Forest [5]. They work with local indigenous communities and small farmers to source organic, fair trade yerba mate while using a shade based growing system in the forest to minimise erosion, protect the soil, quality, and life of the plants [5].

### 3. Cascara 'Tea'

This beverage is often referred to as Coffee Cherry Tea which, given what we have already discussed regarding definitions, is quite a confusing name. Although this is derived from the skins of coffee beans that are sundried until raisin like, many put its flavour profile somewhere between tea and coffee. However, this would be a form of fruit infusion if not considered to be a form of coffee. This is because it is made from the coffee bean husks which is part of the Coffee Cherry fruit. It would be interesting trying to define the beverage if you tried to mix these coffee skins with tea leaves in some way. The beverage is made in coffee producing countries such as Bolivia but has been made around the world under many names; cascara is the Spanish word for husk, but in Yemen, their version of the drink is called Qishr and in Ethiopia is called Hashara [7].

## 4. Cacao Husk Fruit infusion

When making chocolate, cacao (or cocoa) beans are harvested, fermented, and dried. The outer shell of the cacao bean is a fibrous husk, and these are taken when the nibs are separated from the husks, following the cocoa beans being cracked [2]. Like Cascara, these fibrous husks act as the 'leaf' of this fruit infusion. A cacao husk infusion supposedly has a flavour profile similar to that to a dark chocolate. Cocoa beans come from the cocoa fruit and so in this case, labelling this beverage a fruit infusion is appropriate. This beverage was supposedly first consumed by the Mayans in spiritual ceremonies, and so has its origins in South America. However, cacao husks are not heavily exported from South America and only accounted for 0.77% of the global Cocoa Husks, Shells, Skins and Waste exportation globally in 2019 [13].

## 5. Acai Berry Fruit Infusion

The purple acai berry of Brazil is a known super fruit. While many have created tea-like infusions using the fruit, it is also sometimes combined with green tea to add flavour. Health benefits shown when studying extracts of the acai berry fruit included:

1. Antioxidant action,
2. Antihypertensive effects,
3. Anti-diabetic effects,
4. Anti-obesity effects,
5. Cardiovascular & Renal Protective Effects [14].

## 6. Guayusa Herbal Infusion

Guayusa is another South American beverage that has rapidly grown in popularity in the west in recent years [3]. A cousin to the more famous Yerba mate, it is another caffeinated holly tree-based beverage, made from the Ilex Guayusa tree as discussed prior. Guayusa is a product that is primarily produced and consumed in Ecuador [3] and while Yerba mate is a naturally occurring tree to the Atlantic Forest in Brazil, its cousin Guayusa, is found natively in the Amazon rainforest. According to a study that compared Ilex Guayusa & traditional Camellia Sinensis tea, Guayusa exhibits comparable antioxidant & anti-inflammatory properties and has been attributed to be a "good source of dietary phenolic compounds" [6].

## 7. Mate de Coca

Coca tea, also known as mate de coca, is an herbal infusion made from the leaves of the coca tree and is drunk in South American countries such as Ecuador, Peru, and Bolivia. It is outlawed in the United States unless the drink is decocainized, similarly to how coffee might be decaffeinated. It is the alkaloids in coca leaves that are used to make cocaine, however the amount that is contained in one cup of this herbal infusion is very low.

There you have it, 7 popular teas & infusions out of South America. As stated earlier, Asia is clearly the largest exporter of tea globally. So, we will spend a little bit more time in the next section discussing the most famous types of tea & herbal infusions in this continent. Unfortunately, I will never be able to discuss them all as one could write an entire book on the variations of tea in China alone, never mind the many other countries that produce teas worthy of mention in Asia. That being said, let's get stuck into it.

CHAPTER 3: AROUND THE WORLD IN EIGH-TEA DAYS

# ASIA
## 13 of the Most Famous Teas

### 1. Keemun Mao Feng

Keemun Black Tea is produced in the Qimen County in the Anhui Province in China. Its local name is Keemun Gongfu or Qimen Gongfu tea [15]. It is a premium tea that has become famous in places like the UK where it used in some English Breakfast tea blends. Only the most premium quality leaves of the tea plant are chosen in the Mao Feng variation of Keemun; the top bud and top 2 or 3 leaves are the ones separated to be fermented [15]. There is also a version that only uses the buds in the tea called Keemun Haoya Black Tea [15]. Other variations include Hubei Keemun, Keemun Gongfu (Congou), Keemun Xin Ya [16].

It has been described to have a floral aromatic fragrance, a mellow smoky flavour with wooden notes and taste evocative of unsweetened cocoa [16]. The cultivar used to produce this tea is called Zhu Ye Zhong.

### 2. Darjeeling Tea

Darjeeling is in an area in India in the state of West Bengal in the Northeast

of India and is found in the Himalayas [19]. The flavours in Darjeeling tea are the result of growing the tea at elevations of 600 to 2000 metres above sea level as well as the soil quality and local climate [19]. Although primarily known for its black tea, there are white and green variations that come from the region as well.

### 3. Longjing Tea (Dragon Well Tea)

This is a green tea grown in Hangzhou in the Zhejiang province and is China's most famous green tea variation [17]. The tea leaves have a bright emerald colour, a sweet flavour, and an appealing long flat leaf. The name 'Dragon Well Tea' comes from the legend that dragons lived by the lakes in the region where this tea was grown [17]. There are many variations of this tea such as Qian Tang Longjing, Xi Hu Longjing, Bird's Tongue Longjing, Pre-Qingming Longjing, Shi Feng Longjing, Mei Jia Wu Longjing, Bai Longjing & Qian Tang Longjing [18].

### 4. Pu-erh Tea

Made in the Yunnan Province of China, this tea comes under the category of **dark tea** and is made from the leaves and stems of the Camellia Sinensis plant. Pu-erh has a few amazing health benefits: Including the possibility to promote weight loss and boost liver health, it has been shown to reduce cholesterol levels in animals. The most exciting studies show that extracts of the tea when put in test tubes have been shown to kill breast cancer, colon, and oral cancer cells [23] [20]

[21] [22]. Specifically, the post fermented Pu-erh tea used in one of the studies was shown to exhibit more potent anticancer activities than the non-post-fermented version [22]. While more research still needs to be done before it can conceivably be used as form of treatment, the promise of future use and development into cures and treatments for various cancers, is in the realms of possibility [23]. Pu-erh often carries a hefty price tag due to the time it takes to post ferment (it can be up to 50 years!). Once the leaves of this tea are processed, they are usually compressed into a variety of shapes to be sold, for example: Mushroom Shape (Maw Gu Toaw), Brick Tea (Juan Cha) (pictured), Bell Shape (Toa Cha), & Cake Tea (Beeng Cha) [24].

## 5. Baihao Yinzhen Tea (Silver Needle Tea)

This is China's most famous White tea and moreover, their most expensive variety. Only the top buds of the tea plant are used to make this tea similarly to Keemun Haoya Black Tea. However, as it is a white tea, the post processing & fermentation period are different. It boasts a fresh wildflower and honey like aroma with a sweet, light, muscat like flavour; it can sometimes also have a citrusy undertone [25].

### 6. Matcha Tea

A Japanese Green tea which is often sold in powdered form and is used in chocolates, coffee, smoothies, iced & hot tea, and many other applications in Japan. Green teas like matcha naturally have high levels of antioxidants. Additionally, it has been shown to have anti-carcinogenic, anti-inflammatory, anti-viral as well as cardio protective effects [26]. It has a very strong, vegetal, grass-like taste which may or may not be to your fancy, it isn't my favourite, that's for sure. But I do love a good matcha KitKat.

### 7. Sencha Green Tea

This tea is a type of green tea is the most popular in Japan. It is produced from a cultivar called Yabukita. Sencha is grown in direct sunlight making the leaves bright green whereas matcha is kept in the shade before harvest giving it a dark green colour. Sencha is made from the stem, shoot, and leaves which are then steamed and pressed before drying [58]. Matcha only uses the top two leaves but are steamed, pressed, and dried as well. The veins are then removed before grinding into a fine powder [58]. Sencha is a very light tea and is not very strong flavoured which is what is good about it. It's subtly flavoured.

## 8. Bai Hao (Dongfang Meiren)

This is a type of Taiwanese Oolong Tea and is known as the Champagne of Oolong teas. It naturally has a fruity scent with a sweet, but nutty taste, bereft of bitterness. Dongfang Meiren means 'oriental beauty' in Mandarin.

This is a unique tea in many regards because it is referred to an insect tea. The leaves that are harvested to make this tea have had to be partially exposed to the tea jassid, which is an insect that feeds on tea leaves. The insect releases monoterpenes into the leaves of the tea when consuming it which causes it to have a honey like taste [27]. While insect tea normally refers to teas that are made from the faeces of insects that have eaten the tea plant, this tea is made from partially eaten leaves. The terpenes released in the leaves by the insect as well as the natural volatile compounds produced by the plant as a reaction to the insect attack, both play important factors in determining the final quality and flavour of the tea [27].

## 9. Assam Tea

From the region of Assam in India, the largest connected stretch of tea-growing area in the world. Assam Tea has a "deep-amber" colour, a malty flavour and is often used in Irish and English breakfast tea blends [30][31]. Made exclusively from the Camellia Sinensis Var. Assamica plant, the variant is named after this region from where it originates [31].

## 10. Tieguanyin (Iron Goddess of Mercy)

This tea has a slightly strange name, the 'Iron Goddess of Mercy' to do with a legend that a farmer and caretaker of a local temple discovered the tea in a dream. This Oolong tea, when brewed, is golden in colour and has a floral, green vegetable flavour with a sweetness evocative of red peppers [36].

## 11. Da Hong Pao (Big Red Robe)

This is the most expensive tea in the world valued around $1.2 Million per kg of tea. Grown in the beautiful Chinese Wuyi mountains of Fujian province, this Oolong tea originates from cuttings of a single group of mother trees [37]. It is these original 'mother trees' that produce the rare tea that is so sought after. Worth 30 times its weight in gold, the reason for why it is so expensive is that, not many of these plants remain [37]. The tea is made from a rare pure version of the cultivar Qi Dan. As a side note, another popular black tea, Lapsang Souchong, not included in this list of 13, is also grown in this region.

## 12. Liu'an Melon Seed Tea

The oval shape of these tea leaves resembles melon seeds, hence the name. This green tea requires the second leaf of the branch and once the central vein is removed, the leaves are pan fried and shaped to prevent fermentation and to dry out the tea [38].

## 13. Junshan Yinzhen Tea

Authentic Junshan Yinzhen, also known as Master Mountain Silver Needle, is the rarest tea in China. Only 500 kg of it are produced each year as harvesting it is limited to 7-10 days per year in early April. Within that there are many other strict criteria meaning great skill is required to process & harvest this tea [39]. It is a form of yellow tea and comes from the Junshan Island in China's Hunan Province [39]. In 1972, when China retook its legitimate seat at the UN, this was the only tea served to the diplomates and in 2006, this tea was selected as a national gift to the Russian president Vladimir Putin. The leaves resemble needles and when put in boiling water they appear to stand up, creating a forest needle effect in the cup [39].

## 3 Traditional Drinks & Inventions from Asia.

The previous 13 were a few of the many teas grown in Asia and only represent the tea in their raw form; there are many more I could have added to the list. Here are a few examples of traditional drinks made in Asia that involve adding things to the tea to create a new beverage.

**1. Karak Chai or Masala Chai**

Masala, meaning 'spices' in Hindi, lets you know the contents of this beverage. This drink is well known in India and has a few interesting ingredients. Firstly, for masala chai, you need a black tea such as Darjeeling or Assam tea, then you can add either whole dairy milk for thickness or, if you want to add some unique flavours and to make the drink plant based; add cashew or coconut milk. Spices such as ginger, cinnamon, clove, cardamom pods, anise seeds, black pepper and sometimes saffron are often used to bring the spiced chai flavour in. Finally, sweeteners such as maple syrup, or honey are used. Masala chai

## CHAPTER 3: AROUND THE WORLD IN EIGH-TEA DAYS

and karak chai are very similar. The main differences are that in Karak chai, vanilla extract is often used, and evaporated milk is used instead of whole milk, giving it that extra sweetness. This drink is enjoyed very cheaply in middle eastern countries like Qatar & U.A.E as well as in India. If you know where to look, you can grab a cup for as little as 20p or 27¢.

Shai Adeni

This drink comes from the Middle East, in Yemen, and the drink is made with evaporated milk. From the coastal city of Adeni, this drink has cinnamon, cloves, cardamom, and sugar. I have mentioned this here as it shares many of the same qualities as Karak Chai.

## 2. Bubble Tea

I couldn't get through this book without mentioning bubble tea which has had huge in success in the west in recent years. It is served both hot and cold and has a huge range of flavours from sweet to almost no sugar. Originating in Taiwan in the 1980s, this beverage often incorporates Tapioca balls at the bottom of the drink. These can be sucked up using a large straw and chewed on, turning this tea drink into a bit more of a meal; that being said, not a particularly healthy one. There is an insane number of variations in this drink from the tea type; black, green or oolong, to whether its drunk hot or cold, to the flavour additives used such as fruit juice and chocolate through to red bean paste, to the variations in tapioca, fruit jellies and exploding juice balls that are placed at the bottom of the beverage.

### 3. Yuja-cha

This may seem odd to some, but this South Korean infusion is essentially Marmalade added to hot water. You heard me. The marmalade is made from the Yuzu fruit which is a citrus hybrid of the papeda fruit [47] that originated in China but was spread to places like South Korea and Japan some 1300 years ago. It is drunk in the winter months and since the marmalade is essentially made from the Yuzu fruit, I'm going to have to put this into the fruit infusion invention category.

## 3 Famed Fruit & Herbal Infusions from Asia

### 1. Kuding

The Ilex Kaushe is another evergreen but <u>non-caffeinated</u> holly shrub and the Ligustrum Robustum is a wax tree species. Both trees can be used to create Kuding which is a form of non-caffeinated Chinese herbal infusion.

## 2. Monk Fruit 'Tea'

This fruit infusion is a sweet beverage. Luohan Guo, is the local name for it and it contains a compound that is 250 times more potent than sucrose. The beverage is very easy to prepare; you wash the monk fruit, cut it in half and place in a pot and bring water to boil and let it simmer for 30 minutes allowing the flavours diffuse. Then remove & discard the fruit. You can then pour out your fruit infusion into your mug and enjoy!

## 3. 24 Flavours

This is a Chinese drink that has 24 unique ingredients in it. Although the recipe is often known for its taste bad, the combination of herbs is meant to give you a medicinal kick. The ingredients are often changed and not set, but some common ingredients used for this herbal infusion are:

- Mulberry leaves,
- Chrysanthemum flower: A colourful plant local to Europe & Asia,
- Japanese Honeysuckle flower: A flower with a honey-esque taste
- Bamboo leaves,
- Gardenia; A plant from the coffee family,
- Dandelion,
- Cogongrass: a form of grass grown in Europe and Asia,

- Luohan Guo (Monk Fruit),
- Agastache Rugosa: the giant purple Korean mint plant.
- Elsholtzia: A Chinese/Indonesian plant belonging to the mint family
- Fermented Soybean: a fermented Asian legume using bacteria & yeast,
- Syzygium Nervosum flower: flowers from a tree native to Australia,
- Microcos Paniculata leaves: A sour tasting leaf from this Asian shrub.
- Ilex Rotunda leaves: a non-caffeinated Asian holly shrub.

In some variations, Camellia Sinensis is added which turns this beverage into a tea with herbal additives but is usually produced without it.

---

This section has hopefully given you an idea for the level of variety and the unending list of teas grown, drink inventions created, and herbal & fruit infusions composed in the continent of Asia.

Now onward to the continent of Africa!

CHAPTER 3: AROUND THE WORLD IN EIGH-TEA DAYS

# AFRICA
## 11 OF THE MOST COMMON TEAS & INFUSIONS

**1. Kenyan Purple Tea**

Purple tea is made from a cultivar of the Camellia Sinensis tea plant in Kenya that emanates a purple colour (TRFK 306/1); it is propagated through grafting and cutting as opposed to traditional seeding. The reason for their tea plants having this colour is that that there is a higher-than-normal level of antioxidants in the tea leaves. This tea was created by the Tea Research Foundation of Kenya 25 years ago and although it is similar to green tea in the way it is processed, it has a sweet plum flavour, without the grassy taste associated with green tea.

Cool temperatures and rich soil help tea plants survive intense sunlight which normally would be too hot and dry for the plant to thrive in [41]. As a result of increased sunlight intensity and prolonged exposure as well as temperature, the leaves retain a higher level of the anthocyanin compound, which is the antioxidant that makes the leaves purple [40]. This variant is generally more resistant to frost, disease, drought, and pests. Interestingly anthocyanin is the same compound that is present in many berries such as the blueberry.

## 2. Kenyan Black Orthodox Tea

Kenyan Tea demands premium prices because of quality. It is monitored directly by KTDA (Kenyan Tea Development Association). Orthodox tea refers to the process of traditional tea production by hand with the aid of machines, as opposed to a fully automated process. Orthodox teas would tend to be drunk independently (not in a tea bag) with a slice of citrus based fruit to add some zest to the flavour.

## 3. Rwandan Tea

Rwandan tea growing began in 1952 where their tea plants filled their hillsides at an elevation of 1,900 to 2,500 metres. Now the Rwandan tea industry is made of approximately 14 factories and 2 major tea projects [43]. Black CTC, also known as Mamri tea, is the main form of tea produced in Rwanda, but other types like Orthodox tea, Green & White tea are also produced [43]. While orthodox teas are known for their layered, bright taste, CTC teas are stronger with bold tastes and bitter notes. Hence, CTC teas are ideal for tea bags and can be drunk with milk & sugar [42].

## 4. Ethiopian Tea

Ethiopian tea is not usually drunk as just loose tea leaves on its own in hot water, it usually has additives. Addis tea is a popular beverage in Ethiopia and is

## CHAPTER 3: AROUND THE WORLD IN EIGH-TEA DAYS

about how the beverage is prepared as well, not just the tea. Cloves, cardamom, cinnamon stick, and ginger are used to make this beverage which gives the tea a spiced flavour; this is also typically drunk without milk. Another example of this is Shahee which is a drink that is very similar to Addis.

### 5. Ethiopian Mint Herbal Infusion

This can either be drunk straight as an herbal infusion or added to green gunpowder tea or other beverages. All variations are done in Ethiopia. The mint leaves in Ethiopia are grown in a volcanic area called the rift valley at a height of around 7000 feet, and produce smaller, more potent mint leaves than European mint [46].

### 6. Red Rooibos

One of the most popular herbal infusions in the world currently due to it being a sweet flavoured as well as naturally de-caffeinated. This South African drink started 300 years ago amongst the Khoisan people. This infusion comes from the leaves of the Aspalathus Linearis plant [45]. The process of making rooibos starts with planting in seed beds and after the first rainfall, they are

transplanted [44]. The branches are cut and bound into bundles to be processed. It is cut into lengths, bruised, watered, and left to oxidise into a red brick colour which is why it is referred to as red bush by many. It is then dried in the hot sun. These would then be processed in a factory according to their grade and quality. The final steps are screening, then blending and finally a steam treatment [44]. These are then packaged into tea bags and loose tea packages forms. The main allures of rooibos, other than its taste, are:
1. It is high in antioxidants,
2. No additives: it is a completely natural drink,
3. The plant is naturally low in Tannin,
4. The leaves are non-Caffeinated [45].

Red bush reigns supreme in our household and it is a go to after dinner beverage as it has no caffeine and is quite refreshing due to its sweetness. Yorkshire Tea, Earl Grey, Karak chai, Green Tea are also often drunk in our household too.

<u>Vanilla Rooibos:</u> An invention from the red rooibos plant. It is essentially the same red bush infusion with Bourbon Vanilla added in during the post processing steps to give a warm sweet vanilla flavour.

CHAPTER 3: AROUND THE WORLD IN EIGH-TEA DAYS

## 7. Maghrebi: North African Mint Tea

Tea was supposedly first introduced into North Africa by British Merchants who brought over Pingshui gunpowder tea, another Chinese green tea, into Algeria & Morocco during the Crimean War. This was then mixed with mint and sugar to create this beverage, Maghrebi. It is a beverage that was originally local to countries such as Tunisia, Morocco and Mauritania but has now spread as far east as Libya and Egypt. To enjoy this tea authentically, you need 2 main tools: Use a traditional decorative tea glass such as the *keesan*, or *helab*. The second tool is a *Berber*, which is a cast iron teapot with a cone shaped top.

## 8. Green Rooibos

Green rooibos is the less oxidised version of red rooibos as it is given less time to air. If red rooibos is the equivalent of black tea for this species of plant, the Aspalathus Linearis, then green rooibos is the equivalent of green tea for this plant. This too, as with red rooibos is an herbal infusion when added to hot water. It can be bought in loose, or in tea bag form.

### 9. Honey Bush 'Tea'

The cousin to rooibos, the honey bush infusion is made from the leaves of the honey bush (*Melianthus Major*) and is sweet in flavour just like rooibos. The beverage is local to South Africa and the evergreen shrubs are grown in the southwestern cape of SA. Fun fact: when the leaves of this plant are crushed, they give off a peanut butter like aroma.

### 10. Egyptian Chamomile Tea

This is a simple herbal infusion using chamomile petals grown in Menia, Fayoum, Benisuef & Assuit in Egypt. Chamomile is also known to be a mild sedative which can be useful if you struggle with sleep.

### 11. Moringa 'Tea'

Nicknamed *miracle tea*, this plant originates in India & Nepal but is also currently being grown in many places in Africa. However, since Asia has been featured enough, I thought I'd sneak this one into the Africa section. It is technically an herbal infusion as it comes from the Moringa Oleifera tree also known as the 'tree of life'. Its miraculous characteristics are associated with it anti-cancerous properties as well as its anti-diabetic capabilities [94] [95]. The plants leaves are very high in nutrition, providing a variety of vitamins & minerals with a wide range of vital antibiotics and antioxidants as well [94] [95]. Some use these plants leaves for weight loss, but I am unsure of the scientific research to back any weight loss capabilities. It has a very grassy taste reminiscent of matcha green tea. This is especially true when you buy it in its powder form as its appearance is like matcha too. I don't love the flavour of moringa but have gravitated towards it due to its supposed health benefits in hopes it will give me a health kick. Often honey is added when drinking to counteract its grassy flavour.

# Europe
## 8 Teas and Blends common to Europe

Interestingly a lot of the tea grown in Europe is in the region near the Black Sea, For example Georgia, Sochi in Russia, Rize in Turkey, & Lankaran in Azerbaijan.

### 1. Gorreana Orange Pekoe Black Tea

From the oldest plantation in Europe, Gorreana, a region in Portugal brings forth many different grades of teas of both black and green variety but is well known for their Orange Pekoe Black tea, a fine grade of black tea that only uses the terminal bud of the tea plant and its first leaf [48].

### 2. Georgian Tea

Tea grown in this region of Eastern Europe is unique in many respects. Firstly, it is organic; because the tea plants here are not subject to the same pests as in the East which means the tea doesn't require treating with harmful chemicals before it reaches the end consumer. It is also of high quality and rich in flavour, because it comes from plants that are over 50 years old and are seed grown [49]. Also, with the climate in Georgia, only 7 months of the year allow for harvesting the tea plants which gives plenty of time each year for the tea plants to recover and this will enhance the tea flavour and nutrients when harvest time comes around again [49].

## 3. Azerbaijan Tea

Grown in the area of Lankaran by the Azeri and Talysh people, Azerbaijan has a rich tea culture. Men drink tea from Armudu (pear shaped glasses) in tea houses known as Chaykhana, where they read newspapers and play games of backgammon [50]. The tea grown here is black & green tea and is often sold as tea bags in the form of black tea with bergamot (a citrus fruit), or green tea with jasmine for example.

## 4. Rize Tea

Turkey, well known for its coffee is, to no surprise, very big on tea also. Grown on the eastern Black Sea coast, the tea grown here is predominantly Black. Armudu glasses are also used in Turkey to drink tea, but they use a teapot which is more similar to the Russian style of tea drinking. They use a double stacked kettle where they boil water in the bottom one and create a tea concentrate in the top pot with tea leaves in it. It is typically drunk very strong in Turkey and the bottom water filled kettle is to dilute the tea concentrate according to each person's preference. Interestingly, Turkey drinks the most tea per capita in the world according to statistics in 2016, around 6.96 pounds per person [51]. If 1 pound of tea produces around 181 glasses, that is the equivalent of 1,260 glasses of tea per year per person which is 3-4 glasses every day.

## 5. Krasnodar Tea

Many are not aware that tea, which normally requires a mild climate to grow, is being grown in Russia. It is called the world's most northern tea and is grown in the tea-planting village of Solokh-Aul near Sochi in the federal subject of Krasnodar Krai. Black tea is the most common in Russia to be grown with green tea being the second most common. One plantation in Sochi also grows Oolong as well. Although tea was first introduced in Russia from men who visited China, these tea plantations that sprung up have survived the Soviet Union and continue to operate.

## 6. Russian Caravan Tea

Russian Caravan tea is a tea blend. It is blended using Oolong tea, Chinese Keemun tea, and Lapsang

Souchong tea which are at least 2 out of 3 imported, if not all [53]. In the 18$^{th}$ century these teas were imported via camel down the transcontinental 'Great Tea Road' from China to Europe [53]. The flavour profile of this drink which is now enjoyed all over Europe is described to have a sweet and smoky taste [53].

## Zavarka

Zavarka is essentially Black tea (local or not), or Caravan tea but prepared with the Russian style and method. First, you bring water to boil in the Samovar vessel (pictured), then you make the tea concentrate. To do this you add many tea leaves to a teacup or teapot vessel which sits on top of the Samovar [52]. The high tea leaf to water ratio creates the tea concentrate. Alternatively, one, might boil the tea leaves in the hot water at least 5 minutes before putting concentrate direct into the pouring teapot. Here is where you might add any sugar, jams, or additives to the concentrate if you wanted. Finally, the tea is dispensed from the teapot/teacup into everyone's teacup. The samovar dispenses water via a valve tap and each person dilutes the strength of the tea concentrate according to their preference. Of course, this is a traditional method, and most people will just use a teapot & electric kettle to do this today.

## 7. English Breakfast Tea

One of the most famous types of beverages is in fact not a special type of tea but in fact a blend of teas imported from all over the world including Assam and Darjeeling in India, Ceylon (Sri-Lanka), and Kenya. While places like Cornwall in England have recently taken up the mantle of tea growing again, some of the most famous brands such as Tetley, Yorkshire Tea, Twinings & PG Tips mainly import the tea and blend them in the UK.

## 8. Earl Grey Tea

Named after Earl Charles Grey who, in his political career served as Prime Minister of the United Kingdom, this beverage is another popular British beverage [54]. Earl Grey's origin story has had several theories thrown about but, to me, the most likely theory is that the tea was an accidental creation when black tea leaves from China were shipped on an envoy to the UK beside some bergamot oranges [54]. According to this theory, the tea leaves absorbed the flavour of the oranges creating a unique flavour in the tea which is now enjoyed all over.

CHAPTER 3: AROUND THE WORLD IN EIGH-TEA DAYS

There are a few different versions of Earl Grey. Some blends obtain their black tea leaves from Indonesia instead of China. Others like Lady Grey, a trademarked beverage owned by TWININGS, is a variant of Earl Grey that uses lemon peel as well as orange peel in the flavour profile. Vanilla is another additive sometimes added to Earl Grey to enhance the flavour profile.

---

Finally, in our journey across the continents we come to the last 2 continents yet to explore their teas and infusions, Australia & Zealandia. Don't expect Antarctica to be featured in this book unless you are big on iced tea...

## Oceania
## 6 Popular Teas, Blends & Infusions

Most people have never heard of the 8th continent of the world Zealandia, a submerged continent about half the size of Australia that incorporates the landmasses of New Zealand and other surrounding islands. Together, the Australian continent with Zealandia form this sort of geopolitical area recognised as Oceania. Let's look at some of the teas, blends, and infusions from these final two continents.

<u>Australian Tea history, briefly...</u>

Tea was first brought over by members of the first fleet from the United Kingdom in 1788 but was later properly imported in 1794. It was in the 1890s the first tea plantation in Bingil Bay, North Queensland was established by the Cutten Brothers [59]. Being that close to Asia, many Australians also enjoyed Chinese tea, Sri-Lankan, and Indian tea [59].

I particularly enjoyed the humorous recount of the Australian historical tea drinking culture conveyed by Arthur Gray in 'The Little Tea Book' where an average Aussie would, on Monday, <u>without changing</u> the previous day's tea leaves, repeat the process of adding water to their pot hung over the fire. Repeating this Tuesday, through to Friday, by the end of the week the tea's colour is reminiscent of rusty iron and is both very bitter and quite repulsive to most palates. The native Aussie, however, might smile and assert the brew was a "real good old post and rails", considering perfectly brewed, this bitter, rusty tasting beverage [33]. Now... following that detour, let's get into the teas, blends & infusions from Oceania.

## 1. Australian Black & Green Tea

Most Australian grown tea is black with some green tea being produced. The area that produces the most tea is the tropical rainforest zone in North Queensland called Nerada. Approximately 90% of the tea grown in Australia is grown there due to the climate [60]. The biggest name in the Australian grown tea industry is Nerada Tea.

## 2. Australian Breakfast Tea

A rival to the English Breakfast Blend, this Australian invention is made using a blend of Darjeeling, Assam and Ceylon (Sri-Lankan) tea and is a popular favourite in Australia. Other Australian breakfast teas consist of a blend of two or three Australian grown black teas as well.

## 3. Sweet Sarsaparilla Herbal Infusion

Made from the plant native to Eastern Australia, the Smilax Glyciphylla is an evergreen climber that has non-caffeinated leaves [63]. The native aborigines used this plant's leaves in medicinal drinks. This beverage was also adopted by the First Fleet that arrived from the U.K [63]. This drink can be made from the root of the plant or from the sweet leaves.

### 4. Manuka Herbal Infusion

This is a New Zealand beverage made from the leaves of the native evergreen tree called the Manuka tree or *Leptospermum Scoparium,* and has a sweet, floral, and spicy flavour [64]. Bees that feed on this tree, are known for producing quality Manuka honey [64].

### 5. Kawakawa Herbal Infusion

Kawakawa (Macropiper Excelsum) is a shrub which has dark green heart shaped leaves which in the Māori culture, is the symbol for fortitude and courage [61]. There are other variants of the plant on surrounding islands like the 3 King's Island. This infusion can also be made using the root or leaves of the Kawakawa. The fruit of this tree resembles a carrot and is known for its diuretic effects.

### 6. Zealong Organic Tea

This is tea grown from the region of Waikato in New Zealand and is exclusively grown on the Zealong tea

## CHAPTER 3: AROUND THE WORLD IN EIGH-TEA DAYS

estate. Zealong have created a range of 12 teas & infusions that incorporate not only their organic teas but also other additives. While they produce, Black, Green and Oolong tea, just a few examples of their interesting creations are their own breakfast blend and spiced chai, their Lady Gatsby Infusion using Manuka, Cinnamon & Rose, and finally their Lemongrass, Jasmine & Kawakawa infusion called, the green heart blend [62].

> ### A Special Mention
> Alas, we have come to the end of our global exploration of teas, blends, and infusions. From here on out, it will all be practical information about growing your own tea at home. Before we move on, I wanted to feature one of my friends' villages briefly.

<u>Nilai tea:</u> This tea is a special type of green tea produced in the village of Talui in the Ukhrul district, Manipur state, in North-eastern India that borders Myanmar. The unique flavour that is associated with Nilai Tea is to do with the way it is prepared. The tea leaves are double boiled before consuming. This will also decrease the caffeine content in the beverage.

Nilai tea is also hand processed which is another allure.

> Some photos of tea from my friends' back garden in Talui.

## Chapter 4
## Teaming With Life: How to Grow Tea

The ideal conditions for growing tea will always be from whence it originated in China. Thankfully as I have demonstrated in the previous chapter, it has managed to be cultivated and harvested in all variety of weather conditions from the snowy regions in Southern Russia to the tropical climates of Rize, Turkey & Kenya, even the Himalayas. This chapter will start by looking at the ideal conditions for growing tea first, then will move on the practical information on how to get growing...

### The Basic Ideal Tea Growing Conditions

<u>Sunlight</u>: 2-3 hours of sunlight per day with dispersed sunlight either by overcast weather or intentionally grown shade trees.

<u>Soil pH</u>: Maintaining your soil in the range of 4.5 - 5.5 is ideal for tea growth.

<u>Temperature</u>: If your micro-climate is 13-26°C in spring & summer, this is fine, but 18-23°C is ideal as discussed earlier. Extreme temperatures will require extra precautions.

<u>Soil texture</u>: Not too dry, thick with natural nutrients but also drains well.

CHAPTER 4: HOW TO GROW TEA

<u>Water</u>: High mineral water is ideal for rejuvenating the soil. Checking pH of water is good to ensure it's not too acidic or alkaline and is changing the soil pH without you knowing.

<u>Wind</u>: no strong winds to no wind is ideal. This isn't essential but ideal.

If you are unable to provide the ideal conditions stated here, fear not, the sections following this one should deal with your queries related to your specific circumstance & help you get started. This section will give you the general process for growing tea as a starting point.

<u>Growing Timeline & When to Grow</u>

It is a good idea to start out with a macro timeline perspective on tea growing. Provided your microclimate has 4 distinct seasons yearly, you want to be planting your seedlings in late Fall/Autumn, as this is when the tea seeds are usually ripe, and it will be three months later that the seedlings will be ready to have their own pot. From there, count 12 or so months later and that is roughly how long you will need to wait before the plant is ready to transplant outdoors.

We want to be aiming for planting outdoors just as we are coming into spring, so the plant gets the most sunlight and warmth in its initial months outside. So, if you plant your tea seed near the end of November in the U.K or in America for example, you are looking at transplanting it outside mid-March time the following year. Spring & Fall will be dependent on where in the world you are reading this book from. Also, you may not choose to plant from seed, in which case you will need to adjust the timeline accordingly.

### Finding the right location

Now you have an idea of the planting timeline, you will need to think about preparing a suitable location to plant your tea in advance or at least have some idea of the size requirements. Since this is conditional to your living situation, this will depend on the space available to you. If you are living in a flat, you will have no choice but to opt for pot or container-based gardening, either inside the flat or on your balcony, if you have one. Some do build raised beds on their balcony using sleepers, or old pallets. I recommend a very large pot to allow the plant to grow wider and roots to have enough room.

## CHAPTER 4: HOW TO GROW TEA

Choosing the place to plant the tea is key. The camellia sinensis likes sunlight dabbled with shade and if you can find a spot in your garden, yard or balcony that gets 2-3 hours of direct sunlight per day, that is the ideal spot for it. Although you won't be planting your tea plant outside for a while, it is important to have an idea of where it will go when the time comes. The height of the plant will be around 5 foot, or 1.5 metres, so ensure the space you have is sufficient. The plants will be spaced in rows at approximately 4 feet or 1.2 metres between rows, and 2 feet or 0.6 metres apart between each tea plant. Keep this in mind so you can work out how large the area needs to be for the number of plants you want to grow. If your garden is small, it's perfectly fine to half the size between rows. Just be aware that the plant will grow in width when we prune it.

The purpose of the rows is merely to help you walk between the plants when it comes to harvesting. I would not go much below 0.6 metres between plants, otherwise you won't be able to grow your plants very wide. Another alternative is to double up the tea plants and then have a walk row. See the drawings on next page.

When scouting for a place to plant your tea, pay attention to where the wind patterns in your garden or plot of land are, if there's a tendency for it to come from a particular direction e.g., from the side gate, or if you have a city centre garden by the docks for example, the area your garden is in could be a wind trap. Determine if you will need to use some form of permanent wind breaker to protect your plants when they finally make it into the garden or if you need to put them in a green house or poly tunnel permanently.

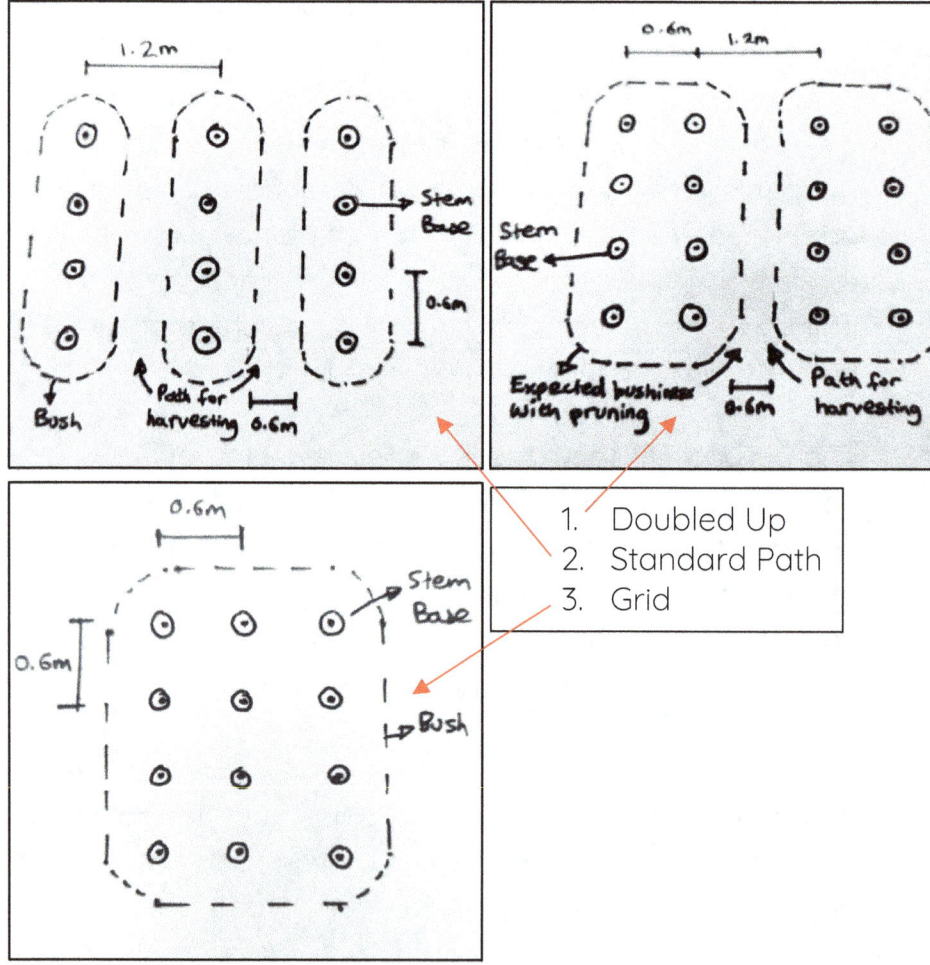

1. Doubled Up
2. Standard Path
3. Grid

## Methods of planting

If this is your first-time gardening, buy some gardening gloves as they will come in handy in their lifetime, not only when planting but when harvesting and removing weeds or for any future projects for example planting vegetables, or medicinal herbs. You will also need some shears to do cuttings, pruning, for de-weeding etc and a trowel.

**Method 1: Growing from seed**

Step 1: Buy the seeds

You can buy tea plant seeds from a garden centre or online. If you live near a plantation, they may have a shop as well.

Step 2: Clean the seeds (optional)

If you feel it necessary, you can clean the seeds with alcohol to kill off any diseases or germs that could affect the tea plant. Rinse the seeds thoroughly after cleaning.

Step 3: Soak the seeds

Tea seeds are relatively large and come with a hard shell. I recommend sitting your seeds in a bucket of water for 24 hours prior to planting. At the end of the

24 hours, hopefully all of seeds will have sunk to the bottom indicating they have greater growing density inside them. If any of the seeds float, this could indicate that the seed may not do as well, however we will plant all of them to keep track. Separate the floaters from the seeds that sunk. If you are doing this with a large number of seeds, try adding a wet towel to the top of the bucket of water to ensure all the seeds are exposed to moisture in the 24 hours.

Step 4: Dry the seeds

Next, we need to dry the seeds out. It is during the drying period that the hull of the seeds begin to crack. In order to control this, you could place the seeds on a **wet** towel or cloth to slow this down. Put a tarp or large dish under neath the towels to prevent water going everywhere. You could spray water over the seeds every 24 hours then leave the seeds for 24 hours to dry. Exposing the seeds to multiple drying and soaking cycles like this, will help the shell to crack. Do this over a period of 3-4 days adhoc depending on how fast they begin to crack. To know how much cracking is enough prior to planting, the crack should be at a tip of the seed and about half a centimetre in length as a very rough guide.

While drying the seeds, sort through the seeds to ensure none of the seeds have any white flesh from

# CHAPTER 4: HOW TO GROW TEA

the plant left on them. This will rot in the ground during germination so remove these from the drying pile.

Step 5: Prepare the soil & germination containers

Next, we need to create a growing mixture for the seeds and use some pots for them if you have between 10 & 20 seeds. If you have 100 + seeds being planted I would recommend using a large plastic container either a cement or paint mixing tub or a gastronorm container; both of which are fairly inexpensive. Ideally use any wide metal or plastic box/container that you already own that will not rot, as opposed to buying something new.

You will also need a Poly Carbonate or Perspex Sheet to cover the box; Whatever you use, it should be transparent or translucent. Cling film may work too.

Also, you will need a minimum of **two** containers, one for the **floater** seeds and one for the **sinker** seeds. Alternatively, you could segregate half of a large container to each seed type. If you do this, make sure you label it in some way. For the soil germination mixture, you can use either a 50 | 50 soil to sand mixture if you would like or if you want to be safe, go all soil. You will be able to reuse the soil later. *N.B. the pH of pure sand is neutral (pH of 7).*

## Measuring the Soil pH

You should measure the pH of the soil prior to planting and aim for a pH of 5.5; standard topsoil will be in the range of 5.5 to 8.5. Even if it is only slightly acidic, e.g., 6 - 6.5, it is better than alkaline soil (7.1+). The most organic way to make your soil acidic is to use compost, however this takes time and does not give you as much control. You can also use an organic liquid feed to control the soil pH. Ensure the acidity is no less than 4.5.

To measure the pH of the soil, use a soil pH meter or some basic soil strips. The soil strips method requires distilled water to be mixed with the soil then drained through some filter paper. You then place the soil strip in the filter solution. If you don't want to buy either of these, then there are basic experiments you can do at home using your soil, white vinegar and baking soda which will tell you if your soil is either acidic, or alkaline, but it won't give you an exact pH reading. The exact soil pH is not as critical in the germination soil but is more critical in step 8 & 9 for when seedlings are planted in their own pot. For the germination soil, just ensure the pH is 6.5 or less.

**Step 6:** Plant seeds in Germination container.

Once the soil and containers are ready, put in some of your soil or soil/sand mixture into the bottom, a few inches of it. Then place the floater seeds in one container (or a few pots) and cover the seeds in an inch of soil or soil mix. Do the same for the seeds that sunk to the bottom of the water bucket and make sure you label which ones are which as it will help you see which plants are most successful later down the line. It is fine to have multiple seeds in one pot or container. They only require just enough space between each other, so the seeds are not touching. The seeds only need enough space to germinate. After 3 months the seedlings will get their own pot.

**Step 7:** Water regularly but don't overdo it.

First you should water the soil using a spray nozzle bottle then conceal the box with your transparent or translucent cover. Keep the box or container in a cold box or greenhouse to maintain warmth and humidity and to ensure the seeds don't get exposed to heavy rain. If you have neither of these, it may be worth buying or building one. However, you could keep the boxes in a conservatory which is well lit and relatively warm. If none of these are available, consider growing them indoors during this period using heat lamps or air conditioning to maintain the room temp around 23 °C. The seeds should start to germinate within 2-3 months in the cold box or greenhouse.

During this period, regularly check on the condensation level on the see-through lid. If the condensation is evenly spread across the entire lid, that is ideal, and it doesn't require further watering yet. If the condensation is not evenly spread on the cover, or if there are large patches where there is no condensation, the soil beneath that area needs further supplementing with water.

Step 8: Seedling Planting

Once your seeds have sprouted into seedlings, you need to transfer them to their own individual pots to grow for their first year. Do this when the seedlings reach a height of 3 to 4 inches or 8-10 centimetres. The pot you should use should be about the size of a 12-ounce cup as this will let it grow to be big enough for final transplanting outside. You can either use plant pots or 12-ounce plastic drinking cups, any container of that sort of size, but preferably one durable enough so that it can be reused in the future. Another option is a hadopot also known as a polypot,

CHAPTER 4: HOW TO GROW TEA

which is a polyethylene bag which is used like a grow bag. Whatever container you use, ensure it has <u>drainage holes</u> for water in it.

Again, the soil mix should be around the 5.5 pH mark, you can use compost or organic liquid feed to bring this down by increasing acidity.

When first transferring your seedlings into their new home, if the roots are twisted and start bending at funny angles, feel free to prune them using your shears to a length of about 2 inches or 5 centimetres before placing them in their new pot.

For the first year of each of your tea plant's life, you will need to keep them in a green house, polytunnel, a tall cold box or indoors using heat lamps to let them grow to a height of 8 inches or 20 centimetres before they are ready for the outdoors. However, if you weather is windless, and relatively mild, feel free to try the placing the pot outside to see how it fairs exposed to the sun & elements.

<u>Step 9:</u> Transplanting final tea plant outside

Once the plants have reached the required height, prepare the ground you want to plant them in. The spacing between rows of tea plants should be around 4 feet or 1.2 metres. Spacing between plants should be 2 – 3 feet or 0.6 - 0.9 metres or as seems best in your garden layout. You should de-weed the soil prior to planting and if possible, dig a trench down about a metre and lay some permeable membrane or fabric down which will help prevent new weeds from coming through, then back fill it with your de-weeded or fresh soil and compact it. The soil should be generally damp, not too dry. The hotter climate you are in, the damper you want your soil to be as this will cool the plant. If using new soil, clay cleat mixed with sand is a good option, just make sure the soil will be able to drain sufficiently when it rains. Don't forget to measure the pH of your soil before final planting. You may only need to treat or check the pH once or twice a year. Now that your soil and location are ready, use an Auger drill to create the hole for the year-old seedling, that is, <u>if you own one.</u> If you don't own one, manually use a trowel (pictured on previous page), to create a hole at 1 - 1.6 foot or 0.3 - 0.5 metres deep. Now you can transplant your tea seedling into the hole. In America and the United Kingdom, the ideal time to plant your tea plants outside is mid-March /early spring. Once the tea plant is in the ground you should supplement the soil area with mulch and organic fertiliser. The reason I push for organic everything is that bad farming practises lead to over soil acidification. Furthermore, mulch consists of dead, organic material made of wood chippings, dead leaves, etc. you can probably use some dead leaves from the sidewalk on your street. It acts as a

## CHAPTER 4: HOW TO GROW TEA

protective covering when you add this on top of the soil your tea is planted in. It protects it frost in the winter, helps retain the moisture and keeps it cool in the summer, and generally protects from unwanted weeds as well.

*Pro Tip #2: If you are planting on a slight slope in your garden or land, then create moats of soil around the plant to capture rainwater as it travels down the slope.*

Water your plant regularly if your area does not have a lot of rainfall.

<u>Maturity:</u> From start to finish it's about a 2-year process until you can harvest your first tea leaves for use, which is about a year after the year-old seedling is first planted outside. After 5 years the plant will really start producing a lot more good quality tea as it will have been pruned to generate many new shoots. Should you choose to keep the tea plant in a container for its lifetime, choose a large container that lets the roots spread out as when you prune it later, the plant will widen to become more of a bush.

*Pro Tip #3: If you live in a cold & windy area, using wind breakers during the winter is advised to protect your precious tea plants from damaging gusts. A research paper on the subject showed plastic film wind breakers increased the heat localised around the tea plant, which although it slightly decreased moisture retention in the plant, it better protected it from low temperatures & winter winds [57].*

## Method 2: Growing tea from a seedling

Purchasing a pre-germinated seedling & transplanting it into a pot to grow for its first year is another way to go about growing tea. If you choose this method, you skip the initial hassle and 3-month wait. Follow from step 6 onwards and your results should be the exact same.

## Method 3: Growing tea from cuttings

Tea is grown all over the world and if you happen to live in a region that is a particularly large grower and exporter of tea, then you may find opportunity to obtain cuttings from a tea bush and plant them in your garden. Alternatively, if you bought a mature plant, or if you have been successful in growing from seed/seedling and want to grow the number tea plants you have, you could use cuttings from your own plants. Cuttings will be a clone of the existing mother plant whereas, each seed produces a slightly different plant because its characteristics are as a result of how it was pollinated.

<u>Selecting the correct mother bush</u>

You want to pick a mother bush to get cuttings from with the characteristics you are looking for, as the cutting will fundamentally be a clone of its mother. A few things to look out for is that the mother plant has a high yield of quality pluckable tea leaves, and the branches are healthy and robust/thick enough for adverse weather [72]. If the exact cultivar is known, choose one that is drought/pest resistant and that roots easily in different soil conditions [72]. The mother bush should ideally be pruned for the 6 months prior to the cuttings being taken for new tea plant propagation [72].

<u>Where to cut</u>: Knowing where to cut is key. You need to cut it on a branch just below where the branch turns from green to brown preferably at the nearest node. Cut on the brown side using garden shears at a 45° angle. Some plant cuttings can be grown using a pot of water to grow out the roots. However, tea cuttings do not thrive in these conditions, they don't like 'wet feet' and so the process for tea would be a little different. First, you want to soak the cutting in an antifungal mixture to prevent any transfer of fungal disease [72]. Then, you'll need a soil mixture as detailed in Step 4 and a pot for each leaf from the cutting.

Next, starting at the top of the cutting, cut each leaf off as you reach the next leaf branch junction (the node). Once you have all the leaves with their branch stems, dip each stem into a growing mixture. You can use inorganic or organic accelerated growing mixture depending on your desired result. Once you've dipped it in the mixture, plant the end of the leaf stem in the soil mixture at roughly 45°. Each leaf should have its own pot, as if you're successful, all these leaves will become tea plants. And Viola! Hopefully, all your leaves will take root and begin growing turning into their own tea plant. Don't be disappointed if they don't all survive, just try again. Watch how much you water it while it's taking root; spraying water using a nozzle rather than pouring might be beneficial just to keep the soil damp. You don't want to drown the plant.

Once you have grown these out for a year or so in a green house, or warm room indoors, follow along from Step 9 just the same!

**Method 4: Buying a mature tea plant**

This is the easiest method as it only requires you to follow step 9.

## Maintaining & Pruning

You will need to continually maintain your plant from weeds, prune it if required and check for frost damage and pests etc. You should prune branches that are growing toward the main stem or are heavily twisted or damaged. This section will not go into detail on pests but refer to the pest section in Chapter 6 to know what to look out for.

To obtain a strong tea bush, you will need to prune your young tea plant strategically to get the shape you require and one that is ideal for harvesting tea. Ideally you want a low, broad, & heavily branched bush that produces many new shoots [72]. The first step is called decentering (see illustration) [72]. Tea plants have a main branch which they grow along, and you want to cut this when 10 leaves are reached on the main stem i.e., cut the top off at the tenth node. This will stimulate the plant to grow secondary, lateral branches. These lateral branches will eventually begin to grow their own leaves also. You then want the plant's lowest secondary branches to grow ten leaves before again cutting the main leader stem again. This will encourage further secondary branches to develop. After you have 4 main secondary branches, you want to prune the bottom 2 lateral branch main stems when all four branches have 10 leaves or so. This may encourage tertiary branches to grow. Keep doing this for the higher up secondary branches and even tertiary branches depending on how fast your plant grows. Doing this will encourage the plant to grow wide & low and will have many branches for harvesting.

Eventually your tea bush will reach a height of 0.5-0.6 metres or 1.6-2 feet with multiple lateral branches and hopefully some tertiary branches too [72]. This is a good height to be your harvesting line or 'plucking table' [72]. The leaves on the new shoots that protrude above this line can be harvested/plucked for making tea. This harvesting line will inevitably grow higher with time. Ultimately you can make the call on how tall you want the tea plant to be and how many branches you want it to have. The more patient you are, and the bushier it gets, the stronger it becomes and ultimately, the yield of tea will be higher. But on the other hand, there will be more plant to monitor for disease & pest.

Do what is manageable for you. Harvested & processed tea can be stored yes, but there is no point in producing quantities of tea largely beyond what you would consume unless you are thinking of commercialising it in some way. More on this later. Furthermore, if you've planted in rows & spaced the plants correctly as well as pruned it to be low and wide, the tea plants may eventually join to form rows of tea bushes. This will take time & patience of course.

During this period of pruning, growth & regrowth, you should keep the soil damp & full of nutrition. View your tea plant as a hungry adolescent eating out the whole house. If the plant has just been pruned, it will also need adequate sunlight, so avoid intentional shade during these periods. It is important during this period to be extra vigilant for disease or pests attacking your plant (see chapter 6). In terms of **when**, typically you would do a yearly prune after the blooming period of the tea plant which happens in Autumn time. However, the intentional decentering pruning operation should be done in early spring, so it has the spring & summer sun to recover and regrow in. You don't want to do this major operation just after it have been planted outside either. My suggested timeline from seedling/cutting to end is detailed on the next page (if growing from seedling start from (1), if starting from a bought plant, start at (2)):

> **Timeline for growing tea**
>
> (1) Indoor/greenhouse plant from seedling/cutting (1 year) ➔ (2) Transplant outside in spring (1 year) ➔ (3) Mild pruning that Autumn of flowers & general maintenance ➔ (4) The following spring, if it has reached the 10-leaf requirement, perform the major decentering prune ➔ (5) Depending on how fast it regrows you may be able to prune again at the start of summer (Avoid major pruning just before winter) ➔ (6) Continue pruning as detailed above in the following spring until happy with height & number of branches etc.➔ By year 3 or 4, you should have a nice, low, wide tea bush that produces a reasonable amount of new tea shoots for tea harvesting ➔ Some pruned branches can be used for making tea.

Before you first perform the major decentering operation on your tea plants, it may be worth waiting until they reach 13 or 14 leaves and then cut the major stems down to 10 leaves. That way, the 3-4 extra leaves you have just cut off your tea plants can be bundled together and used in your first tea batch. If you have only planted one isolated tea plant, these leaves won't be enough for a batch of processed tea but may be enough to create a single cup of unprocessed white tea.

CHAPTER 4: HOW TO GROW TEA

<u>Decentering</u>: This shows an illustration of 1st major pruning operation the plant will undergo. You prune the plants in the 2nd spring outdoors and the same mid-summer if it has regrown sufficiently. Then the following spring & summer and so on.

The end result should be a low, wide & dense tea bush that yields many new shoots ready to be harvested when they grow above the harvesting line. All the new growth above this line is harvested & used to produce tea in the 1st, 2nd and 3rd flushes of the plant.

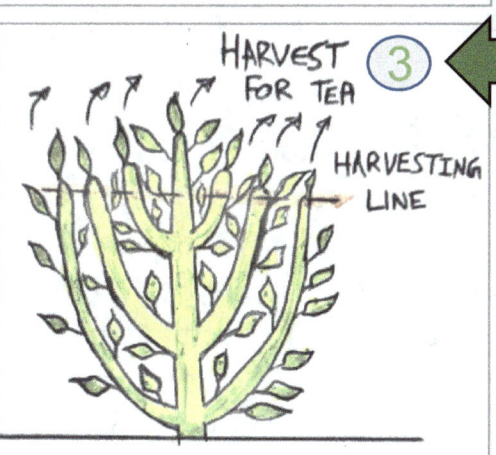

Please note, images 1-3 only show pruning cycles to help stimulate the secondary branches to grow. To encourage growth of the tertiary branches, you need to repeat the same process steps 1-3 but by pruning the secondary branches instead of the primary branches. i.e., prune the secondary branches when they reach above 10 leaves etc.

### Formative Pruning

After 6 years, when the harvesting line has reached 44 inches (1.2 metres), tea bushes normally require a mass pruning where all the branches are pruned to a height of 18 inches (0.45 metres) from the ground [72]. This instigates a mass rejuvenation in the plant. Again, massive pruning operations should be done in early spring so they can recover in the sun of spring and summer.

## Growing Tea in Any Climate

In this book we have so far covered what the ideal conditions are for growing tea in terms of temperature, light conditions, and soil pH, as well as the process of growing from seed etc. If you live in extreme climates such as summers over 40°C or winters less than 0°C, have heavy wind or rainfall, then this section is for you.

Extreme heat: I recommend either starting from a pre-purchased grown plant or cutting if you are growing in extreme heat. If you start from cuttings, I would grow them mostly inside with the help of UV growing lamps or by manually moving the potted tea plant outside for a few hours a day, but not in the peak sun. I lived in the U.A.E for 18 years and so I understand that not much can grow in the summers

# CHAPTER 4: HOW TO GROW TEA

there where the heat can reach over 50°C. However, the winter in the U.A.E boasts temperatures of 15-28°C which is ideal for tea growing. In such a climate, I would want the tea plant outside during the winter and inside during the summer. If you keep the tea plant in a *small pot* for the rest of its life, it won't be able to grow and be pruned into a more bountiful bush. However, if you have a few plants on the go, you may be able to produce sufficient tea for your home needs. If you are confined to container gardening, I'd recommend a very large and deep pot about 1 m deep and about 60 cm wide to give it room for its roots and a secure base for when the plant is widened. If you have a large enough garden there are various ways you can keep the plant cool in the blistering heat:

1- There are Desert based technologies to keep plants cool in a separate structure without the need for constant air conditioning. In the Dubai sustainable city for example [97], they have bio domes which contain fans that blow air out of the structure creating negative pressure inside the dome where the plants are grown. They have windows covered in permeable fabric that are constantly wet with grey water produced by the city. The negative pressure causes air from the outside to be sucked in through the permeable fabric and, because the fabric is wet, this naturally cools the dome and keeps the plants at a temperature that can sustain their existence. While you will require a fan or two to get this going, it is a very simple system if you are willing to do a bit of DIY. Such a system could be retrofitted to an existing shed or greenhouse even. This is vital to keep plants going in 40°C heat or higher. Of course, you can grow plants in the house with you, but you will be limited in space. An external structure like this will allow you to grow many different types of plants. The fan can also be run on solar power.

2- If grown in an outdoor building, having a metal ceiling on the inside will allow the water to condense and rewater the plants rather than most of it escaping. Painting the outside of the structure in UV reflective paint will decrease the heat absorbed by the structure from the sun.

3- Next, keeping the soil cool is key to plant survival in the blistering heat. Mulch will protect the soil from heat and help retain moisture.

4- Use Shade Trees. These will keep the plant out of the peak heat most of the day and, if planted right will allow for only 1-3 hours of diffused light on the tea plant.

Extreme cold: Green houses, Polytunnels and Cold boxes are your go-to for keeping plants warm in cold environments. However, in some winter climates the plant would still be too cold. Your options are then limited to artificial heating or moving your plants indoors during part of the year which is not ideal as it requires your tea plant to be permanently potted. Watering with warm (not hot) water will help too; Using mulch on top of the soil will protect the soil from freezing and choosing the right cultivar from the get-go can also help prevent frost. You can use heat lamps to aid in heating during this time as well as wind breakers if your plant is outside, braving the elements. Just so you know, heat lamps can't be used to grow the plants as they don't emit the right wavelength of light for that. You would need a grow lamp or a UV lamp for that.

Extreme rain: With great rain I would recommend installing proper drainage in your garden & soil that drains adequately. As well as this, raised beds offer a better drainage solution than ground beds. Furthermore, if the rain is excessive, I recommend sectioning off/walling off the area you are growing your tea plants in. During heavy rain, I would use some form of artificial cover such as an outdoor umbrella or canopy to prevent the plant being damaged from the force of the rain and the soil becoming flooded. The walling you build around your tea nursery, if deep enough, will help protect it from the soil around it that is receiving the excessive rainfall. Cheap concrete blocks are one of the cheapest ways to build retaining walls.

Extreme wind: Greenhouses are a great way to protect from strong wind, Polytunnels may not be sturdy enough. Wind breakers may not stay up in very strong winds. Again, you always have the option of growing indoors. Intentionally planted trees can act as wind breakers in your garden too.

Over acidic/alkaline soil: Again, instead of replacing all of the soil in your garden, utilising a raised bed would enable you to purchase different soil with the right characteristics rather than using the poor-quality soil you have naturally in your garden. However, you can still treat the soil in your garden and get it to the right pH using organic and inorganic chemical sprays as well as compost. Getting new soil is the easier option.

Limited space: If you live in an apartment then you will have to grow your tea plant in pots. If you have a large enough balcony, you could build a raised bed out of pallets and sleepers. You would need to make sure you have some form of tarp down and drainage solution in place for when you water the plants. You may be able to sustain your needs with one or two pruned wide low tea bushes that are producing may new shoots, but this is optimistic. If you do grow your

# CHAPTER 4: HOW TO GROW TEA

plant permanently inside, ensure there is adequate ventilation to control the humidity and temperature.

## How frequently to water the soil?

In the first 2 years you want to water your plant 2 to 3 times a week if there is no rainfall where you are. About once a week after that unless you have a lot of rain, in which case check to see if the soil around the plant is damp weekly. In warmer or desert climates, you may need to do this more often if the water gets evaporated quickly, so you need to be attentive and play it by ear. In the period directly after major pruning operations, water it a little more regularly but don't overdo it.

## Harvesting & Processing foreword...

After about 2 years (~1 year of being outside), your Camellia will be a mature enough plant to harvest some tea leaves. Some of the pruned leaves & stems can also be used for tea rather than wasted. Once your tea bush has undergone major pruning and bounced back, it will then really be producing a lot more harvestable tea. The simplest teas to produce at home are black tea, green tea, and white tea. I recommend harvesting with the intention of processing these particular types, at least initially. Nevertheless, in the next section I will list all 6 types along with where & what you need to harvest in order to make them. Before we enter the next chapter, it is important to note that there are many variations within each tea type which might change the method, order of processing or the specific post processing technique used, the temperatures, the no. of cycles as well as <u>when</u> or <u>which</u> leaves are picked. For example, most yellow teas have no rolling step whereas a few specific types of yellow tea <u>do include</u> a rolling step. What I've tried to do in the next section is provide the generic process for making that tea type rather than go into detail about every different variation, as this will just be too much information. Once you have mastered the 6 generic tea types you will then be able to move on to experimenting with the processing steps and hopefully attain varying results in taste, flavour & aroma.

CHAPTER 5: HARVESTING, PROCESSING & STORAGE

## Chapter 5
## Harvesting, Processing & Storage

The basics of <u>harvesting</u>: You can use gardening shears to cut off new shoots or pluck them hand. You can cut the tea leaves anywhere from the node (where the stem branches off), to where the stem reaches the leaf. Generally, people cut at the nodes.

Top quality teas only use the terminal leaf/bud and top two leaves which contain the most flavour and caffeine, however I recommend harvesting at least the top 3 leaves and the terminal bud of the shoots that grow above your harvesting  line to maximise what you get out of your plant. You want to harvest the tops of each major shoot of this bush, where new young leaves have just sprouted. You don't want the leaves you harvest to be too mature. If you haven't undergone decentering, you will only have the one major shoot, as new secondary or tertiary branches have not been encouraged to grow yet. This is why pruning is important. When harvesting, I recommend cutting the shoot off with

Cut at the node below third leaf

123

shears or plucking by hand but to do this at the top of the node above the 4$^{th}$ leaf. That way you don't *leaf behind*, excuse the pun, a load of dead stems. See the red line on pictures on the previous page for where to harvest on the tea shoot. The picture above is an edited version of the original used with same attributed reference [74].

If you want to have a go at making Lapsang Souchong or other teas associated with the fourth leaf down from the terminal bud, then, by all means, harvest the fourth leaf as well. Once you've collected the tops of these shoots, you can either keep or remove the stems for processing. This is up to your preference but generally, the highest quality teas will not include the stems.

# CHAPTER 5: HARVESTING, PROCESSING & STORAGE

## Ways to Harvest

> Selective harvesting (recommended): This would be if you only intended to harvest ripe leaves [69]. Whether they are young or old is up to you, but the younger leaves are associated with quality.

Non-selective harvesting (not suggested): The removal of all shoots including immature (not ripe), dormant, mature & overmature shoots [69]. Endlessly harvesting all shoots will degrade the plant over time.

> Coarse Plucking (recommended): More than 2 leaves. Up to 4, but I have suggested 3 leaves & the bud. You can harvest the 4$^{th}$ as well if you intend to make Lapsang souchong as I mentioned before [69].

Fine Plucking (necessary for some teas): Removal of 2 of the leaves & bud. Used for the finer teas such as Flowery Orange Pekoe or high-quality green teas [69]. (Note: the best teas only use 2 leaves & 1 bud)

My recommendation is either a combination of coarse or fine plucking & selective harvesting. I wouldn't advise taking all types of leaves and shoots for making tea, but feel free to experiment and see what the lower down or immature leaves taste like too. A lot of this whole tea making process is understanding the basic principles and then, once these are mastered, a lot of experimentation and playing around with the growing, harvesting, processing and final tea recipe to end up with a tea or beverage that is truly unique in taste and aroma.

To apply the information above practically, once your tea bush is both wide & has multiple branches, you can create a plucking line. Feel free to label this on the plant with a ribbon or have a pole or plank in the ground beside the bush to indicate the height of the plucking line. Any new growth above this line is what you will harvest for tea. You would be harvesting at the node of the leaf stem once 3 leaves and a terminal bud have formed above the plucking line across all the new shoots. Note down the frequency of how fast it grows back ready to be harvested again. In spring, this regrowth time should be faster but will likely slowdown in the summertime.

# CHAPTER 5: HARVESTING, PROCESSING & STORAGE

## Processing the 6 types of tea at home

**White Tea** is harvested from the youngest leaves in spring. Pluck/Snip the top two leaves and bud from the harvested shoot and whither the tea leaves by letting them sit in open air for about 7 hours or overnight. And that's it! White tea has no further post processing. It is the simplest to harvest & process. The final step after this is storage.

**Yellow Tea** is made using leaves harvested in early spring as well.

Basic Process: (1) Picking➔ (2) Withering➔ (3) Separating ➔ (4) Steaming/Frying ➔ (5) Smothering ➔ (6) Final Drying

(1) Depending on the type of yellow tea you are making, you will either be using just the terminal bud or, both the stem, top two leaves & the terminal bud. (2) Whichever you decide, you need to wither the buds/leaves for 2 hours in direct sunlight, or 5 hours in the shade, on bamboo mats. Do not use violet-coloured buds or any leaves damaged by insects or frost [84]. You will be able to repick these in two weeks' time but the closer to summer you pick the leaves, the lower quality yellow tea you will get. (3) Next, the leaves are placed in a rotating drum with a grid to allow through only leaves of consistent size. Seeing as you will not likely have a rotating drum this can be

## CHAPTER 5: HARVESTING, PROCESSING & STORAGE

done through a colander or large sieve. If the holes are too big on your colander, you can use tape to make the hole size consistent. Alternatively, you could separate the tea leaf sizes into piles by hand. Be sure to remove broken leaves. Although one set size leaf is often used for yellow tea, it is better you just create different batches of yellow tea using different size leaves and store them separately to minimise waste. (4) Next, you need to steam the bud & leaves for 2 minutes at a temp of 180-200°C [84]. This is the easiest method, but the most traditional method is to wok fry <u>small quantities</u> of tea leaves in a triangular motion on the pan at a temperature of 120°C for a few minutes, then on to the edges of the wok at 90°C for a few minutes [84]. If you choose this method, fry the <u>small quantity</u> batches of leaves according to leaf size. (5) The final step of yellow tea is the special step that differentiates it from green tea. It is referred to as smothering or 'sealing yellow'. Take your leaves and place them on a cloth or towel and cover them in the same cloth or towel. Once this has sat for 24 hours, slowly roast the leaves again for 2 hours at 26°C, then take them out the oven and re-smother in the cloth for another 24 hours [84]. Do this 3 times which will be take around 72 hours. This should turn the leaves a yellow golden colour as micro-oxidation takes place over the 3 days [84]. (6) The final drying step: Place the tea in the oven for 20 mins @ 100°C. Then store.

**Green Tea** uses a similar process to yellow tea except without the need for the bamboo mats, and the final smothering step. Additionally, green tea can also be made using leaves lower down the plant. Stems can also be used when making matcha tea. Furthermore, instead of the smothering step used in yellow tea making, there is a rolling step that occurs after the leaves are cooled after steaming/frying. Steps 1-3 are the same as with yellow tea.

Basic Process: (1) Picking ➔ (2) Withering ➔ (3) Steaming/Frying ➔ (4) Rolling ➔ (5) Final Drying ➔ (6) Extra Processing (e.g., grinding)

(4) Rolling: Use a table, large container or a clean, tablecloth covered floor as your rolling station. To perform hand rolling grab a large handful of tea leaves between your hands rub your hands together letting the tea fall back onto your rolling station. Then grab a large hand full of the leaves and rub your hand together again. Keep doing this with repetition. Simultaneously, roll the tea on the rolling station surface by hand, clumping it together into large rolls or balls & pushing it across the surface, then disbanding it from its clumps using the hand rubbing method again. You are

meant to press these balls as if trying to squeeze out of the tea leaves moisture. Do this for 30 minutes. The leaves should then be ready for final drying. Some plantations do further cycles of heating & rolling before final drying. (5) Final drying involves placing in the oven for 20 minutes at 100°C. A big differentiation within this process occurs depending on if you want to make a Japanese or a Chinese green tea. Chinese green tea is characterised by pan/wok frying for step (3) whereas Japanese green teas use steaming, both are standard options. (6) To make Japanese Matcha Tea, you must not only have used the steaming method in step (3), but as a final additional step you must grind the dry leaves into a powder; this is normally done using granite grinders.

**Oolong Tea's** export market is led by China & Sri-Lanka. It requires a fermentation step that green tea doesn't, but is never fully oxidised like black tea. Lightly oxidised oolong tea is 5-40% oxidised whereas heavily oxidised oolong is 41-70%. It has a basic grading system from common oolong to the highest quality; extra fine.

---

Basic Process: (1) Picking ➔ (2) Withering ➔ (3) Bruising & Partial Fermentation ➔ (4) Frying (Fixation) ➔ (5) Rolling ➔ (6) Final Drying

TEAMING WITH LIFE

(1) Pluck the top 2 or 3 leaves and terminal bud from the camellia sinensis, and use these. These should be mature leaves, not too young, the difference will be made manifest in the end tea taste. At the point of harvesting oolong, the bud should be about half the size of the leaf. If you have multiple cultivars or are harvesting leaves at different times of the day or are picking leaves of different maturity, then separate these into piles to make different batches of oolong so you can control the quality. (2) You wither the leaves outside in the sun for 30 minutes and bring them inside to cool. You then turn the leaves over and put them outside again for 30 minutes. You then repeat the turning, sun-withering, and cooling 4 times. If the sunlight is weak compared to the ambient temperature, an hour or more per period of sunlight exposure may be required. If you have no direct sun, use a solar lamp indoors, maintaining the lamp temperature around 30-40°C. Make sure the leaves don't exceed 40°C. You will know visually that the tea leaves are ready by the loss of vibrance in colour; they will also appear wavy. There may also be an aroma beginning to be released. The weight of the leaves will have reduced by about 10% due to evaporation of water in the leaves. If you weigh the tea before, this can be a metric by which to determine if the tea is ready for the next step. (3) The next step is

132

## CHAPTER 5: HARVESTING, PROCESSING & STORAGE

to bruise the tea leaves. Once the last withering cycle is over, bring the tea inside and place on bamboo mats inside (or a tablecloth). Let them sit to cool for 1-2 hours, then you can initiate the first bruising/shaking cycle. This is very simple. You essentially take the leaves and turn them over each other by picking them up and dropping them (not from height) on to the other leaves round and round. Do this for 5 minutes and then let the tea leaves sit again, for 1.5 hours in a room at 25°C. This bruising process, which is a much gentler version of the rolling process, should be done 3 to 5 times. This is where the partial oxidation of the leaves occurs and turns a brownish golden colour. The final rest period should be 2 hours. (4) After this, you need to wok fry the leaves in the pan at a temperature of 120°C for a few minutes, then on to the edges of the wok at 90°C for a few minutes, as with yellow tea. Doing this will inactivate the oxidation process in the leaves and 'fix it' in place. Next, we have the rolling and shaping step. The way this is done in industry is to wrap 9kg of leaves into a ball in a large cloth & put this into a machine to bruise & squeeze the leaves juices out. (5) At home, I'd suggest the same rolling process as with green tea, making sure you squeeze out those tea juices to the outside of the leaves as you are rolling them by hand. Another home method

133

is to wrap the separated piles of tea into balls in a tea cloth and do the pressing & rolling of the balls by hand that way. (6) The final drying stage achieves a final fix of the oxidation process. Do this in an oven at 100°C for 20 minutes.

**Black tea** (Red tea in the East) is made using the top bud and the top 2 young leaves on the plant. I will only show you how to do the process for making Orthodox tea at home, not the CTC method.

Basic Process: (1) Picking ➔ (2) Withering ➔ (3) Rolling ➔ (4) Fermentation ➔ (5) Final Drying

(1) Plucking Black tea is dependent on the type of tea you are making. Go to the tea grades section to see which leaves are used for which grade of tea. Assuming you are making a standard orange pekoe grade, you will need the top bud & first two leaves. (2) The withering process is similar to Oolong tea, except with more cycles of withering until the tea has lost about 30% of its water weight from its original weight. Again, if you don't have much sunlight, store in a warm room/greenhouse at 30-40°C with a solar lamp. (3) Next step, hand-rolling can be applied again, the same as before. (4) Fermentation done at 25°C is optimum according to this research paper **[81]** but 20-30°C is sufficient. The room it is oxidised in should be kept humid using a humidifier if there is not any

## CHAPTER 5: HARVESTING, PROCESSING & STORAGE

natural humidity. There should be plenty of oxygen to allow oxidation to occur and one should avoid dry air or wind blowing over the leaves. For full oxidation, this process takes about 3-4 hours until fully darkened. No fixation is required as the leaves are allowed to fully ferment. (4) Final drying should be done at 121°C in the oven for 20 minutes.

**Dark Tea** (Black tea in the East) is also made using the top bud and top two leaves of the plant. It is the same as black tea but, prior to final drying, it has a post fermenting step which oxidises the leaves even further. Steps (1) to (4) & also (5) are the same as in black tea.

Basic Process: (1) Picking➔ (2) Withering➔ (3) Rolling➔ (4) Fermentation ➔ (4b) Aging /Pile Fermentation ➔ (5) Final Drying

(4b) Aging can be done to most of 6 tea types and involves letting the enzymes in the tea get to work. Ageing only works well if it has not been subjected to high heat (above 120°C). To age Pu-erh via natural fermentation, you would pile the tea into a mound or form into a cake and cover it with a breathable cloth [82]. This wants to be stored in a humid but cool environment. This process can take weeks, months and even up to 50 years for the finer dark teas. Raw aged Pu-erh tea is very expensive because of this long process and the time required. A faster technique, known as Pile fermentation, is to wet the tea prior to letting it age which activates the microbial fermenting of a fungus agent called Aspergillus Niger which speeds up the post fermenting process [82]. This method produces what is known as Ripened Pu-erh. (5) Once the tea is sufficiently aged, it is either re-rolled and final dried or just final dried straight away. Step (5) is the same as with black tea but may need to be put in the oven for longer at lower heat to remove all the moisture. When making teas that use microbes to age them, the potential for poisoning oneself is conceivable and, while the boiling water should kill off these microbes upon brewing, it is worth washing the tea leaves in boiling water prior to your first brew [82]. Making your own Pu-erh tea is one for the veteran tea grower I think...

> *Pro tip #4: The bud & first two leaves are the most often used because they have the most flavour. From a biochemical point of view, these three have the most polyphenols & caffeine [81]. This translates to a stronger green tea flavour and, after oxidation, a stronger black tea flavour as these flavonoids turn to theaflavins & thearubigins.*

## Decaffeinated Tea

If you've heard the rumour of decaf tea being made by bleaching tea bags, then truth is not far off. In the late 19$^{th}$ century organic solvents such as benzene, chloroform, methylene chloride, acetone, methanol, and ethanol were used to in decaffeinating processes as well as strong bases & acids such as ammonium hydroxide and sulfuric acid [92]. It was only due to health concerns these substance uses were halted. No Kidding! There are 5 main methods for proper caffeine removal & 1 crude method. I have named & detailed all these below for you.

1- Decaffeination using solvents: The first method uses the modern-day standard organic solvent. Ethyl Acetate is a see-though, flammable, & volatile liquid that has a fruity flavour as it is a substance found in many fruits such as pears & apples etc. It is completely digestible and is used in various foods such as desserts & dressings. It was approved for use in the process of decaffeination by the US FDA in 1982 [92]. Once you treat the tea with the ethyl acetate, the caffeine gets extracted from the tea leaves into the solution. Then you need a 1% Citric Acid Aqueous Solution to extract the caffeine from the solution. Concerns with this process are to do with toxic residues left behind.

2- Decaffeination using $CO_2$: This method involves first grinding down the tea until the pieces are no more than 1 mm in width, then the powder is then soaked in an ethanol/water solution to extract the caffeine from the leaves [92]. This solution is then loaded into an extraction vessel where carbon dioxide is pumped through the chamber to take the caffeine away [92]. Although the process requires expensive equipment, it is very fast, leaves no toxic residues behind and retains a high amount of the tea's flavour [92]. You obviously couldn't do this at home but it's interesting to know none the less.

3- Decaffeination using Water: Water decaffeination is done by blanching (the process of immersion in a hot/boiling liquid) the freshly harvested green tea leaves in boiling water for a short period of time. Boiling water will cause the caffeine in the leaves to be extracted faster than the catechins associated with tea flavour. After blanching, you then remove the tea leaves from the caffeinated water and dry the tea leaves. This process may seem simple, but in fact it's like removing that first brew of the tea leaves which will contain most of the caffeine. Thankfully this process can be done at home by anyone. The optimal conditions of this

## CHAPTER 5: HARVESTING, PROCESSING & STORAGE

process are 100°C water, blanching period of 3-4 minutes and a boiling water / tea ratio of 20 mL per 1 gram of tea leaves [92]. If this is done, then you can expect approximately 83% of the caffeine to be removed and 95% of the flavour to retained [92]. Although this is not 100% decaf, it is pretty close. However, these are the ideal conditions for processing the first four leaves of the shoot [92]. Leaves harvested from further down the shoot require a 10-minute blanching period to achieve 80% decaffeination and 85% retention of flavour [92]. Once the freshly harvested tea leaves are blanched then dried, you would continue processing the tea leaves as normal to produce green, oolong or black tea, etc. This is the only method I'd recommend doing at home.

4- Decaffeination using Microorganisms: Certain organisms such as the bacillus licheniformis strain were found to reduce the caffeine in tea leaves when sprayed on their surface [92]. Other microorganisms taken from soil in tea plantations have shown effective degradation of caffeine too [92]. Scaling this up to industry requires more research & development as it has a few variables that require controlling [92]. This maybe a good option for the home tea grower in future but for now requires more R&D.

5- Decaffeination using absorbents is another process that exists but is a complex process that is beyond the scope of this book.

Crude method: Delaying leaf picking period & shortening the amount of post rolling can help reduce the caffeine content in the tea leaves, however it would only be classified as low caffeine and not completely decaffeinated [92]. Certain cultivars are also bred to have lower caffeine. In conclusion, for home growing tea, I would only recommend Method 3 as it is easy to do, requires no harmful solvents or microorganisms, no specialised equipment and is both fast and easy to do.

# CHAPTER 5: HARVESTING, PROCESSING & STORAGE

## Storing your tea

This is the final step for all your tea types once final drying has occurred. For the fermented teas, they are often formed into cake like shapes for storage which involves compressing e.g., brick or disc shape etc. In general, if you are storing your tea loose or in cake form, you need to find an opaque container in a dark cool room that is not humid at all. Avoid putting it near items with strong odours as tea easily absorbs flavours and smells. Make sure you label your teas, you may have different batches of tea depending on leaf size, when you harvested them etc, so make sure you label everything and don't mix them together. Every so often, check on your stored teas to ensure they haven't gotten damp where they are being stored as it would be a shame to ruin all your hard work at this point!

In general, all the tea types will age a little, even when they are being stored, specifically white tea, green tea, and Pu-erh due to the enzymes still being active in the leaves. Oolong tea can be further aged if you re-roast the leaves every few years or so [83].

# Chapter 6
## Pests, Diseases & Cultivation

There are many bugs, insects and birds that will be interested in your tea plants. You need to know which to disturb and which to not. Don't disturb a hummingbird if it decides to make a nest in your tea plant. It won't harm the plant but will likely pollinate and eat pests as will some spiders that love to live in this plant. The presence of ants can be neutral or negative thing, they may not feed on your plant, but they do often protect pests which are feeding on your plant. However, if those pests are not present, the ants may well be harmless.

## Pest Management

There are four main ways to manage pests,

1. Cultural deterrents: to prune the leaves damaged by pests or stems/leaves home to insect eggs, intercropping, weed control, using pest resistant cultivars [72].
2. Manual deterrents: removing pests manually, de-weeding, water-jetting etc,
3. Biological deterrents: introducing pest predators such as parasites, spiders & fungi into your garden can help control pest populations [72],
4. Chemical deterrents: your last resort should be using pesticides, insecticides, and other chemicals. Sometimes though, it's necessary.

## Tea Pests & Deterrents

### White Grubs

These C-shaped grubs feed on the roots of plants and turn into beetles when mature. See image on right [93]. Their eggs are laid  from March to June in the peak tea plant season and begin to emerge late summer. They can move between plants so beware if you find them in one place. They can cause damage to your tea roots which can make the upper leaves & branches dry. They grow in manure so if you are using this as a fertiliser, make sure it has decomposed sufficiently before applying. Chemical Control measures include neem extract or a pyrethrum-based pesticide. If you want to introduce a biological deterrent, I recommend Beauveria Bassiana, a type of fungus [72]. This deterrent can also be used against the tea mosquito as well. Hit two bugs with one stone.

### Thrips & Mites

Black Thrips, Yellow, Purple, Red & Scarlet Mites are all examples of different versions that can attack your tea plant [69]. They generally live on the underside of leaves so make sure you inspect these regularly [69].

Each type of mite or thrip causes different issues in the plant such as darkening or browning of mature

leaves, leaves turning purple & bronze, etc. These major tea pests feed on the sap in the leaves and stem. They are small but large in number and thrive in humid conditions. The tea leaves will become matte or curled and may yellow at the edges due to less sap being present in the leaves. Manual control measures including spraying the infected plant with a jet of cold, high-pressure water (not too strong so as to damage the plant) [72]. This should be done for three days. Another option is to prune the infected branches or leaves. Chemical control measures include insecticidal soap mixed with water in a spray bottle, or Miticides which, to no surprise, are intended to kill mites specifically [69]. Another option is Spinosad spray [72]. Use these sprays after dark, so you don't affect any honeybees [72]. Keep applying these measures until all larvae are gone.

Tea Mosquito

Another major tea pest are these sap suckers so try & avoid them breeding. Biological measures such as Beauveria Bassiana are available in powder form

## CHAPTER 6: PESTS, DISEASES & CULTIVATION

and should be mixed and applied correctly whilst wearing the correct safety equipment. These types of natural insect fighter are better for the soil, the tea plant, and any vegetables you may be growing rather than the chemical-based pesticides which so often find their way into the food chain. Another deterrent to the tea mosquito is the smell of burnt tea leaves which is an easy one to try.

### Shot Hole Borer & the Sapling Borer

These are another major tea pest. The prior is a black beetle and the latter a grey moth. Symptoms of the prior are holes in the primary branches, death of buds, circular tunnels in the major stem, structural weakness, death of plant [86]. Symptoms of the latter may include chewed areas near the branch collars of the plant. Use pruning as a manual procedure for helping alleviate the problem but, if this does not work, you may need to remove and dispose of the entire affected plant(s) as borers are highly invasive and difficult to remove [86]. Don't use fungus to treat this problem as these can help the borers invade the plant by weakening it structurally. Save as many plants as you can from being affected, as even one of these borers can take down a whole plant with time. Borers love to eat bark so make sure you inspect any nearby trees in your garden as well as the mulch used for the soil prior to planting the tea plant and continue to check regularly.

Crickets

This noisy but common garden bug will feed on a variety of plants including the camellia sinensis. They can be particularly harmful in that the crickets will cut off entire stems and eat the leaves. Although they may be more likely to get the lower down leaves which are less wanted it's still a cause for concern. You especially want to avoid them when your plant is in its first year  exposed to elements, when your tea plant is still young. Manual control measures include placing a water trap near the infected area. This can be made with a container filled with water and mixed with Black Treacle (Molasses) [72]. If you are growing your tea nursery is in a greenhouse or poly tunnel, ensure all windows and cracks are sealed. As far as chemical agents go, using the non-toxic, food-grade diatomaceous earth powder, or a cornmeal & boric acid combo will kill crickets, so you can spread one of these on the soil near your tea plant or where you can hear them in the garden. Image reference is [94].

## Nematodes

These are parasitic worms. Some use these to treat white grubs but they can develop into being an even bigger problem themselves as they can form knots around the roots which manifests in the plant being unable to grow very tall and a struggle to produce chlorophyll [72]. Neem cake is an adequate deterrent of this issue. A study showed using a 1:100 (1%) neem cake to soil ratio reduced the root nematodes by 23% on corn roots & by 70% in the soil surrounding the roots [85]. The effectiveness of this was even higher in a greenhouse environment [85].

## Rodents (voles, rats & mice, etc)

You will indefinitely find rodents in your garden at some point in your gardening journey, it's just a matter of when. Whether they have become a major issue is for you to check. Look for rodent holes being dug near your tea plant which could disrupt the roots [72]. Manual control methods include regularly checking round your plant. De-grassing your garden will reduce the rodents in your garden as they prefer to move in grassy areas [72]. Traditional physical & chemical mouse traps are an option too if it is really a big issue. Rodents will be a bigger issue if you are simultaneously growing fruits & vegetables.

## Scale Insects

A serious pest is the scale insects which appear as brown, armoured or shotshell bugs on the underside on leaf veins or on the stems. They can turn the leaves white due to honeydew resin from soft shell kind of the scale insect. They can turn leaves yellow or brown as the leaves ability to produce chlorophyll dwindles [69]. They can also attract black mould when their honey residue rots, but even worse is that the honeydew resin attracts ants that protect the scale insects from their natural predators such as ladybugs and wasps etc. The females appear as small brown fish scales without legs (they camp out in one location on the leaf or stem), and the males are flies which you are unlikely to see on the leaf. To treat scale insects, you can either remove their protection by killing the ants with ant powder or by removing their ability to climb your tea plant by coating the stems in a slippery wax or gel that will inhibit the ants e.g., Vaseline [89]. If you do apply a slippery coating to the stem, blow the remaining ants off the plant and ensure there is no other entry points they can climb the plant [89]. If, after this, the predators do not take care of the scale insects naturally, you may need to consider other options, such as systematic insecticides. These are applied to the roots, soaked through the plant and kill off the scale insects, mites or other pests feeding on the leaves. Such an example is Acephate. However, I am unsure of how this will affect the final tea taste if you apply this close to harvesting time. Finally, you can try homemade remedies such as oil, dishwasher liquid and a lot of water in a spray which smothers the scale insects to prevent it from breathing and eventually dying & falling off.

Tea Jassid

This bug can either be seen as a minor tea pest or a valuable worker depending on your tea tasting preference. But generally, the tea jassid's snacking on the tea leaves will add a honey like flavour to your tea leaves through the terpenes released through its teeth. They can become an issue when they lay their eggs in the leaves or when they eat too much, turning leaves brown.

## Intercropping

Intercropping is a good cultural deterrent as when different crops are paired, they can help one another. This can increase tea yield and decrease pests & diseases. For example, planting lavender near your tea plant, will repel mosquitos. Lavender is also a useful ingredient that is often used in flavouring teas as well as in various herbal infusions. If lavender is not to your fancy, then try lemongrass as this also has mosquito repellent properties. Garlic is an aphid repellent, which is another minor tea pest. Marigolds are known nematode repellents as well as mosquitos, rabbits (the rodent's cousin), aphids (a minor pest), & white flies [87]. Also branded as the Calendula, the Marigold's flowers are often used in herbal infusions and boasts benefits such as skin healing when applied direct to the skin [86]. In addition to this, they have antioxidants & anti-inflammatory capabilities when drunk [86]. Generally, herbs are good at resisting pests. It is always good to have diversity in your garden and to keep your plants healthy. Healthy crops are less targeted by pests than already sick or malnourished crops.

*Pro tip #5: Syrphid flies also help control aphid populations as a biological deterrent if they become a major pest [69].*

## Chemical Deterrents

This should be a last resort. Even so I will only recommend organic options. You can research other deterrents which are not organic readily too. Neem Oil (slows growth of pest population), Bacillus Thuringiensis (a bacteria which can be sprayed on leaves as insecticide as is non-toxic to humans), Pyrethrin (an insecticide), Rotenone (pest and insecticide), Spinosad (soil-based bacterium that fights insects such as borers, worms, mites etc.) [88][72]. There is also Acephate, mentioned prior.

## Tea Diseases

There are a few main diseases to be aware of when it comes to the tea plant.

**Root Diseases:** These are broadly caused by fungi [72]. Your soil needs to have proper drainage otherwise this could be a result. As well as this you need to understand if, during your rainy season, your garden gets flooded with water. If it does, consider installing land drains or additional manholes. If there is a natural slope to your garden, you can install aco drains so the water runs toward to the house into a drain for example. Another way to encourage drainage is to have raised beds, which will add to the total amount of soil in the garden and will ensure the water does go further into the ground. If your garden soil is thick and bad at draining, you will be able to control the soil that goes into your raised bed by purchasing topsoil from merchants or garden centres that has your desired properties i.e., less dense, better drainage, etc.

Black root disease, root splitting disease & red root disease are all examples of root disease [72]. The upper half of the plant will manifest dryness & wilted leaves but in general, it's hard to detect these diseases without root inspection. Once the upper half has been affected, its already too late. Neem cake is a way to treat it but in a lot of cases you'll need to uproot and burn the infected plant [72]. If you do intend to treat the plant, isolate it in a pot and treat. Check the other plant's roots for symptoms too.

**Blister Blight:** A disease caused by a pathogen that thrives in humid conditions, cooler temperatures & low sunlight which is often the conditions present at high altitudes [72]. It can be identified by yellow oil spots on the leaves, enlarged lumps, lesions, & white spore bulbs which turn brown. Infected stems will fall off and die. Cultural control methods include exposing the plant to a long period of sunlight (> 5 hours) and limiting its shade time. Also planting in rows will help prevent the spread of this disease between plants. Prune affected stems or leaves if the sunlight treatment does not cause it to bounce back.

## Cultivation

Some cultivars have been propagated to be less prone to frost and drought, more tolerant to pests and less prone to disease. Some of these include the Kenyan propagated varieties: TRFK 306 (Purple Tea), TRFK 704/2, TRFK 597/1 [69]. The second two are particularly resistant to tea mosquitos. There are

## CHAPTER 6: PESTS, DISEASES & CULTIVATION

many other cultivars to choose from. If you have an issue with a particular pest or a worrying climate related issue, it may be worth trying to purchase a grown plant or seedling of a suitable cultivar or obtain a cutting of one its branches. This will require research to find the right cultivar for you and your situation, but will likely be worth it in the long run.

In short, cuttings are clones of the mother plant, whereas seed grown tea plants will have a mixture of characteristics from the mother plant & the father plant which pollinated it. You can try control this through intentional pollination, but you will never have absolute control over which genes are carried from one plant to the other. If you want predictable results, it is far easier to start with cuttings. I would research the properties of different cultivars, and which might be best suited to your climate. Then obtain cuttings from a variety of cultivars that are suited to your microclimate. Then, when the plants grow & are naturally pollinated by bees & other natural pollinators, the seeds that are eventually produced by tea plant will hopefully have a combination of the characteristics of the parent cultivars you selected. Nevertheless, on the next page I have detailed some basic information for those of you who would like to intentionally cultivate specific plants together at home without fancy equipment.

Cultivation techniques: If cultivation at home is something you would like to try yourself, there are a couple of ways to propagate new cultivars. Mutation breeding is an artificial gene variation producing technique induced by biological, chemical, and physical factors. This is usually done in a lab setting. A second technique is hybridization which is one of most common methods for breeding new varieties [91]. Distant hybridization is a method where you take very different cultivars and breed them. Doing this has the greatest potential to broaden new characteristics and genes. For example, the Camellia Sinensis and Camellia Japonica were bred to produce a hybrid called Chatsubaki, which exhibited higher resistance to specific tea diseases as well as frost whilst having a lower caffeine content in its leaves [91].

Basic plant reproductive morphology: The female organ on a plant is called the Pistil, which is made up of the ovary, the style (stem) & the stigma (the end that is pollinated). The male organ is called the Stamen, made up of the filament (stem) & the anther which is the tip of the filament with pollen on it. There is usually one pistil per camellia flower but multiple stamens. The pistil will usually have one style but can have multiple stigmas branching off the end of it. If the end does not branch off, it will have a stubby end.

CHAPTER 6: PESTS, DISEASES & CULTIVATION

How to breed plants: The basic process of breeding plants is detailed below. First you need to wait for the flowers to bloom. You want to do this just as the flower buds open. Then using a small razor or box

knife, you cut open the flower by carefully removing the petals of the father plant and identify where the stamens (male organ with pollen) are & where the pistil is (female organ central stem). The stamens have pollen on the end. Cut off all the stamen on the flower you intend to be the father plant and leave only the stigma behind (be careful not to let the stamen touch stigma when doing this). Having collected the stamen of the father plant, go to the plant you wish to breed it with and cut off the outer petals. Remove the stamen of the mother plant's flower here too being very careful to not let the pollen of the stamen touch the sigma as this will cause self-pollination. Now you should have stamen of both tea plants you will be able to rub the stamen of each flower on to the stigma of the other. If the pollen does not stick to the end of the stigma you may need to wait a day or two until the stigma is receptive and try again. In the meantime, keep the stigma covered in a permeable nylon bag. After successful pollination, cover the flower again in the nylon bag to signify that it has been pollinated but also to protect it. Pollinate the other plant too so that when the seeds come forth you will be able to see which traits have come from which parent. Cross pollinating both plants may give you a higher chance of producing seeds that eventually exhibit desired characteristics. When the seeds are mature and ripe, they will be a reddish-brown colour and the capsules will have begun to crack open. These can be harvested. Plant them as detailed in Method 1 of the planting section in Chapter 4. If these successfully take root and grow, when the tea plant is mature, you will be able to identify which seed produced more desirable traits and from which parent they got these traits. Make sure you label everything, so you don't mix them up. E.g., label them plant 1 & plant 2. Also label the seeds e.g., father plant 1 - mother plant 2, & mother plant 1 - father plant 2…

CHAPTER 6: PESTS, DISEASES & CULTIVATION

> *Pro tip #6: If you only intend to breed in one direction i.e., reserve 1 plant solely as the father & 1 solely as the mother, then you can take stamens from the father when the flower shows colour, but you don't need to wait for the flower to open before taking the stamen.*

Cultivating this way, doesn't require any specialised equipment or the understanding of the biochemicals in the plant, it can be done by almost anyone. I recommend giving it a go if you have successfully nurtured multiple tea plants already and are looking to try something new.

We have now come to the end of our tea growing journey together. So far, we have covered what tea is & isn't and what the different types of tea are. We've looked at the various plants and fruits used in caffeinated and non-caffeinated herbal & fruit infusions. You should now be well on your way to becoming a tea connoisseur having understood the key components that make up tea quality. You should also now have an idea of the  variety of teas, tea blends, infusions, and beverage creations out there in the world. The list I detailed is of course, inexhaustive. Finally, in the following previous two chapters we have covered, growing, maintaining, & pruning your tea plant to make it a thriving & fruitful bush. We looked at how to process the 6 different types of tea at home, the basics of decaffeinating tea at home and looked at how to store your hard work, so it doesn't spoil. Then, in this chapter we have looked at the pests & diseases covering the main 4 forms of deterrents as well as how to do basic cultivation at home. We have now arrived at the final chapter together! Recipes to make use of all the tea you have been growing!

# Chapter 7
## FORTY RECIPES FOR-TEA

I truly hope that you have been successful on your tea growing journey! I hope your tea plants mature well & produce you much tea. May they be a fine addition to your garden & growing journey. For many of you, this is just the next stage in your self-sufficiency journey. For others of you, this is your first attempt at growing a plant outdoors. Congrats to you either way! This next section will show you what to do with all the tea you are harvesting. In this chapter you'll find many interesting recipes & inventions from around the world from hot & spiced tea, to iced tea, to cakes & savoury dishes, here are 40 recipes to try with the fruit of your labours. Please note, many of these recipes can be done with purchased tea bags too, instead of using your own homegrown tea.

### HOT & SPICED TEA RECIPES

SHAI ADENI (YEMEN)
This beverage is a sweet Middle Eastern tea often enjoyed in Yemen.

Ingredients (serves 2)
4 Cloves, 1 Cinnamon stick (broken)
$1/4$ Teaspoon of Ground Ginger
6 Green Cardamom Pods (press to slightly open)
$1/2$ Cup of Sweetened Evaporated Milk

2 Cups of Water
1 ½ Tablespoons of Black Tea Leaves

Instructions

1. In a saucepan bring to a simmer all the ingredients above except the tea for around 10 minutes. This will allow the flavours to begin to mix and come out. (Ginger is optional).
2. Next, add the tea leaves to the simmering mixture. You will need to continue the simmering for at least another 5 minutes to allow the tea to diffuse into the mixture. Let it simmer for as long as you wish, make it the strength of the tea according to your preference.
3. Taste test & add sugar as required. It is meant to be a sweet drink. Next, filter the saucepan contents into a tea pot & enjoy the beverage!

---

## KARAK CHAI (INDIAN)

Basic karak chai is made using black tea, cardamom, evaporated milk & sugar. However, there are many variations. Here is a common alternative recipe with a few more flavours.

Ingredients (serves 4)
3 Cloves
1 Cinnamon stick (broken)
4 Tablespoons of White Sugar
$1/4$ Teaspoon of Ground Ginger
6 Green Cardamom Pods (press to slightly open)
$2/3$ Cup of Sweetened Evaporated Milk

## CHAPTER 7: FORTY RECIPES FOR TEA

4 Cups of Water
2 Tablespoons of Black Tea Leaves

Instructions

1. In a saucepan caramelise the sugar on its own in a saucepan (don't burn) on medium heat with a tiny drop of water. As this caramelises (turns brown), slowly add the cups of water.
2. Add the tea leaves & spices then bring the mixture to boil. Then let it simmer on low to medium heat for 10 minutes.
3. Next, add the evaporated milk, simmer for a further 10 minutes.
4. After this, filter the saucepan contents into a tea pot & enjoy!

---

### SHAHEE TEA (ETHIOPIAN)

Ingredients (serves 4)

1 Cinnamon stick (broken)
8 Cloves
9 Green Cardamom Pods (press to slightly open)
½ Teaspoon Ground Cinnamon
⅛ Teaspoon Ground Nutmeg
3 - 4 Cups of Water
¼ Teaspoon of Ground Ginger
1½ Tablespoons Tossign (Ethiopian Thyme)

Instructions

1. The core ingredients in Ethiopian tea are very similar to others discussed so far: the cardamom pods, cloves, & cinnamon stick.

1ˢᵗ Method: boil the tea, cardamom pods, cloves, and cinnamon stick ingredients in water for 10 minutes. Filter the tea leaves, pods, cloves, and cinnamon stick, then enjoy!

2ⁿᵈ Method: Blend 2 tablespoons of cloves, 3 tablespoons of green cardamom pods, & 2 cinnamon sticks. This will be your Ethiopian spice mix reserve which you can store in a pot/jar. You can add a tablespoon of this to 3 cups of boiling water with 1 tablespoon of black tea or green tea. Then leave it to simmer for 10 minutes, filter the tea leaves and enjoy!

3ʳᵈ Method: Boil the total ingredients listed above including the thyme, nutmeg, and ginger. This itself can be enjoyed on its own without the tea if simmered in boiling water for 10 minutes and filtered. But add 1 tablespoon of green or black tea to the mix according to preference. Simmer with the tea leaves for 5-7 minutes, filter the mixture & serve.

4ᵗʰ Method: Take the spice ingredients from (3ʳᵈ version) and triple quantities and blend into a powder which you can store and use a spice mix. You can add 1 tablespoon of this spice mix to 3 cups of boiling water with 1 tablespoon of black tea or green tea. Then simmer for 10 minutes, filter the tea leaves out, serve and enjoy!

2. If you are using the spice mix to make your Ethiopian tea (method 2 & 4), then bear in mind you will need to use less when in powder form, as the powder form will be much stronger than the diffusing methods.

# CHAPTER 7: FORTY RECIPES FOR TEA

## MAGHREBI MINT TEA (MORROCON)

Ingredients (serves 6)
5-6 Cups of Water
2 Tablespoons or 1 Ounce of fresh mint leaves
1 Tablespoon of Green Tea leaves or powder
Add Sugar to preference

Instructions

1. Bring water to boil and add ingredients all together. Simmer on low heat for 10-15 minutes. Reserve a few mint leaves for the end.
2. Drain the tea and serve in heatproof glasses. Add the extra mint leaves to the glass and enjoy the beverage.

## EARL GREY (UNITED KINGDOM)

Ingredients (4 - 6 servings)
5 Tablespoon of Black Tea
Bergamot Essential Oil or Bergamot Orange

Instructions: To make this there are two methods. Bergamot oranges are local to North America & Italy so if you have access to some, this may be easier than worrying about using essential oils.

1st Method: Using bergamot oil: You must use a therapeutic grade only. The reason for using 5 tablespoons of black tea is because you would normally make a batch of earl grey and store it. However, you can do this with more, or less tea, at your convenience. Never add bergamot oil directly to water as oil and water don't mix, so it will not dilute the essential oil. Anyway, the method consists of dripping a few drops into a jar and turning and shaking the jar, so the entire inside is coated in a thin layer of this oil. Then put in your loose tea in and shake jar. You want to seal this and store it for at least 3 days, shaking the tea every so often.

2nd Method: Using Bergamot Oranges: Peel the bergamot orange and place the peel in a jar with the black tea leaves. Dampen the tea leaves very slightly so they are slightly absorbent. The tea will absorb the flavours & aromas. Do this for 24 hours but shake the tea every so often to move the tea around to absorb the peel. If making a batch, then you should dry it in the oven before storing without the peel in the jar. This will kill off any microbes. Whenever you want to brew an earl grey tea, prepare it as you would normally for any black tea leaves. It is also quite normal to add other citrus flavours such as lemon peel & grapefruit peel to the mix. Store the dried tea leaves in an opaque container in a cool but not damp location & use as required.

CHAPTER 7: FORTY RECIPES FOR TEA

## MATCHA GREEN TEA LATTE (JAPAN)

Ingredients (serves 1)
1 Teaspoon of Matcha Green Tea Powder
300ml of milk
(1¼ cups of milk)
¼ Cup of Water
2 Teaspoons of sugar

Instructions

1. Add the sugar and matcha powder into a mug.
2. Warm the water to just below boiling and add slowly to the matcha and mix the ingredients into a paste.
3. Warm the milk in a saucepan until near boiling
4. Add the milk to the mug, then whisk the ingredients together until the latte appears a light green colour throughout.

## HOT BUBBLE ALMOND TEA (THAILAND)

There is a Taiwanese version of this tea, but this version uses a special Thai spice mix that gives the drink a lovely bright orange colour.

Ingredients (serves 2)
7½ Cups of Water,
½ Cup of Black Tapioca Pearls,
½ Cup of Turbinado Sugar
(alt. mix: ¼ cup white & ¼ brown sugar mixed)

¼ Cup of Almond Syrup or a ¾ teaspoon of Almond Extract,
½ Cup of Thai Tea Mix,
3 Tablespoons of Black Tea Leaves,
½ Cup of Almond Milk

<u>Instructions</u>

1. Boil the 5 cups of water & add the tapioca balls & boil for 5 minutes. Remove from the heat and let it sit for 10 minutes. Strain before adding to glasses in step 4.
2. While the pearls are sitting, heat a ½ cup of water then mix in the sugar in another pan until it is fully dissolved. Transfer these to a ceramic bowl & stir in the almond syrup /extract. This is now your syrup mix.
3. Using the remaining 2 cups of water, boil them and add in the Thailand tea mix along with the black tea leaves. Let this simmer for 5 minutes then sit it off the heat for a further 2 minutes. Strain/filter the tea into a jug.
4. Prepare the two drinking glasses with half the tapioca balls in each glass. Make sure the glasses are suitable for hot beverages.
5. Then add 1 or 2 tables spoons of your syrup mix into each glass according to preference.
6. Add 1 cup or 240 ml of the hot tea mixture from the jug into each of the glasses. Depending on the size of the glass you may just split the contents of the jug two ways or three if there is enough.

# CHAPTER 7: FORTY RECIPES FOR TEA

7. Split the ¼ cup of almond milk evenly between the two glasses. You can then mix the whole beverage using a spoon.
8. Taste and stir, add more syrup mix as required, and finally, enjoy!

## 5 SPICE LATTE (CHINA)

<u>Ingredients</u> (serves 1)
¼ - ½ Teaspoons of Chinese 5 Spice
(or home-made version),
1 Cup of Water
1 Teaspoon of Honey
¾ Tablespoon of Black Tea leaves
Add Cinnamon for Garnish

<u>Instructions</u>

1. Boil the water with the tea leaves for 5 minutes and strain/filter the liquid into a mug.
2. Add the honey & 5 spice powder and stir. Use honey to taste.
3. Top up the beverage with warm and frothed milk. Use a whisk or milk frother to froth the warmed milk by hand.
4. Finally, garnish the latte with cinnamon & little extra 5 spice powder.

## SWAHILI GINGER & MILK TEA (MOZAMBIQUE & KENYA)

<u>Ingredients</u> (serves 4)
¼ Cup of Grated Ginger
(Alternatively use ¼ cup of ginger powder)

3 Tablespoons of Black Tea
4 Cups of Water
2 Cups of Milk
1/4 Cup of White of Brown Sugar (to taste)

Instructions

1. Boil the Water with the ginger and black tea leaves for 6 minutes.
2. Add the Milk and Sugar and let the mixture simmer for 3 more minutes until all sugar is dissolved. Then remove from the heat.
3. Strain the Black tea leaves & any large ginger bits left using a sieve.
4. Finally serve in mugs and enjoy!

## IRISH WHISKEY TEA (IRELAND)

As with its cousin, the Irish Coffee, this whiskey tea is also quite alcoholic.

Ingredients (serves 2)
1 Tablespoon of Black Tea Leaves
1 Tablespoon of Honey (to taste)
1.5 Shots/Jiggers of Irish Whiskey (66mL)
1/4 Cup of Milk
2 Cups of Water

Instructions

1. Boil the water with the tea leaves for 10 minutes. Strain the tea leaves.
2. Add the whiskey and sugar, stir, then add the milk as required. Serve up and enjoy!

## TEA INFUSED MULLED WINE

Black & Oolong Tea work best for red mulled wine.

### Ingredients
2 Sticks of Cinnamon
3 Star Anise
4 Cloves
5 Tablespoons of Tea Leaves (Black or Oolong)
1 Bottle of your Favourite Red Wine
Lemon Zest from 1 Lemon
Orange Zest from 1 Orange
4 Tablespoons of Sugar (to taste)
$1/4$ Cup of Brandy (optional)

### Instructions

1. Rinse Tea leaves in boiling water to start infusion process.
2. Decant the wine into a large pot. Heat up the wine on low heat. Do not bring to simmer or boil.
3. Add all the other ingredients. Keep it on low heat for around 30 minutes allowing it all to diffuse. Taste every so often, to ensure the tea does not overpower the mixture. Add sugar to taste preference.
4. You can optionally strain the mixture and keep the mulled wine on very low heat prior to serving which will stop the tea diffusing process (do this if it will not be consumed immediately) or you can serve directly using a ladle!

## ZAFRANI CHAI / SAFFRON TEA (INDIA)

<u>Ingredients</u>  (serves 4)

2 Cups of Water
2 Cups of Milk
3 - 4 Tablespoon of Black or Oolong Tea Leaves
35 Strands of Saffron
9 Cardamom Pods (crushed)
3 - 4 Tablespoons of Sugar (to taste)
½ Teaspoon of Black Pepper
1 Juiced Lemon & Zest
4 Teaspoons of Honey for sweetness

<u>Instructions</u>

1. Boil the water and add the cardamom and saffron. Let these boil for 2 minutes.
   (Optional: For extra flavour you can add a stick of cinnamon & lemon zest)
2. Add the tea leaves and boil for 5 minutes then add the milk & sugar and bring to boil. Simmer on low heat for 5-10 minutes, according to your chai strength preference.
3. Strain the tea leaves out and serve in heat proof glasses to enjoy.

---

### Turmeric Tea (Golden Milk Tea)

Normally this spiced beverage contains turmeric without any tea present in the beverage. Another example of misusing the word **tea**. Below though, I have created a modified recipe that includes the use of green tea leaves but feel free to try this without the tea leaves or try with black tea leaves.

CHAPTER 7: FORTY RECIPES FOR TEA

Ingredients (serves 4)
2 Cups of Water
2 Cups of Regular or Coconut Milk
3 - 4 Tablespoon of Green Tea Leaves
1 Teaspoon of Turmeric

Instructions

1. Mix the Honey, Turmeric, and the Black Pepper into a paste in a bowl.
2. Brew the tea leaves in the water for 10 minutes then strain.
3. Add a teaspoon of the honey turmeric mix to the bottom of the serving glasses. Then pour in about half a cup of brewed green tea into each glass. Mix well until completely dissolved.
4. Warm up the whole milk or coconut milk you choose. Do not make hot, only warm it. Then froth the milk using a frother or a whisk.
5. Top each glass with ½ a cup of warmed frothy coconut milk & serve.

---

## RUSSIAN SPICED TEA (RUSSIA)

Ingredients (serves 8)
8 Cups of Boiled Water
5 Tablespoons of Black Tea Leaves
1 Cinnamon Stick
1½ Cups of Sugar (to taste)
1 Cup of Orange Juice
¼ Cup of Lemon Juice
10 Cloves

## Instructions

1. Add the spices, water, tea, and sugar to pan and bring to boil. Simmer on low heat for ten minutes. Then strain the mixture of the spices and tea leaves.
2. After this, in the same pan, stir in the orange and lemon juice heating until it comes to simmer again for about 2 minutes. Then serve immediately!

---

### VANILLA CHAI

Ingredients (serves 6)
4 Cups of Boiled Water
2 Cups of Milk
1 Tablespoon of Vanilla Extract
5 Tablespoons of Black Tea
4 Cloves
2 Teaspoons of Black Pepper
4 Teaspoons of Ground Ginger
2 Teaspoon of Nutmeg
2 Crushed Cardamom Pods
1 Cinnamon Stick
3-4 Tablespoons of Maple Syrup (to taste)
$1/2$ Cup of Whipping Cream
2 Teaspoons of White Sugar

## Instructions

1. Add the spices, tea and syrup to a pan and add the Boiling water. Let these ingredients heat up together. Boil for 2 minutes then let it simmer for

10 minutes. Strain the mixture into a large heat proof jug.
2. Heat up the milk and add the vanilla extract. Once mixed and heated, add this to the jug and mix in the jug.
3. Whip the whipping cream and add the 2 teaspoons of sugar to it.
4. Serve the Vanilla Chai into heat proof glasses or mugs and top with the whipped cream. Feel free to powder the top with nutmeg or cinnamon at will. Enjoy this warm winter drink with friends or family!

## ICED TEA

### SPARKLING OOLONG LEMONGRASS GINGER TEA

<u>Ingredients</u> (serves 4)
4 Cup of Water
1 Lemon (sliced into segments for glasses) (optional)
4 Teaspoons of Sugar
2 Tablespoon of Oolong Tea Leaves.
*Can be done with green tea also.*
8 Mint Leaves
2 Teaspoons of Lime Juice (optional)
4 Teaspoons of Sugar
2 Cup of Sparkling Water
1 Teaspoon of Freshly Sliced Ginger Root
2 - 3 Stalks of Lemongrass
(can be chopped or whole)
Ice Cubes

## Instructions

1. Add the water to the saucepan. Bring to boil
2. Add the oolong tea leaves to the water as well as 4 mint leaves, sugar, ginger, & lemon grass. Bring to boil and simmer for 2 minutes and turn off heat and stir for a further 5 minutes. Add in the lime near the end (optional).
3. Then strain/filter the mixture of leaves and lemongrass.
4. Prepare glasses with a mint leaf in each, then add ice & distribute the sparkling water among the glasses equally.
5. Finally add the cooled tea mixture to each of the glasses. Garnish with a slice of lemon for each glass. Then enjoy!

## MILK OOLONG TEA (TAIWAN)

Ingredients (serves 1)
1 Cup of Water
2 Teaspoons of sugar
1 Tablespoon of Oolong Tea leaves
120ml of milk ($1/_2$ cup of milk)
Ice Cubes

## Instructions

1. Add the water to the saucepan. Bring it to boil.
2. Add Oolong tea leaves to the water and reduce to simmer. Simmer for 5 to 10 minutes.
3. Then add the milk and sugar to the pan. Bring to simmer again.

CHAPTER 7: FORTY RECIPES FOR TEA

4. Once you bring it to simmer again, remove from heat & strain/filter the liquid of the oolong leaves. Let it cool for about 5 minutes.
5. Finally add ice to a glass and pour in the warm liquid. Then enjoy!

---

### MATCHA GREEN TEA ICED LATTE (JAPAN)

Ingredients (serves 1)
1¼ a Cup of Water
2 Teaspoons of Sugar
1 Teaspoon of Matcha Green Tea Powder
300ml of Milk
(1¼ cups of milk)
Ice Cubes

Instructions

1. Add sugar & matcha powder into a mug. Add more as required.
2. Heat a ¼ cup of the water to just below boiling and slowly add it to the matcha & mix these ingredients into a paste. Then add the extra cup of warm (not hot) water and mix. This is your matcha syrup. If it is too diluted in flavour add more sugar & matcha powder.
3. Put this in the fridge to cool & transfer the ice to the drinking glass.
4. Add the milk to the mug, enough until ¾ of the way full. Then add the matcha syrup mixture to top it up. Then enjoy!

## TAIWANESE BUBBLE TEA (TAIWAN)

<u>Ingredients</u> (serves 2)
7 Cups of Water
½ Cup of Tapioca Pearls
1 Teaspoon of Black Tea Leaves
½ Cup of Milk
(118 mL of milk)
1 Cup of Ice Cubes

<u>Instructions</u>

1. First, we need the black tea mixture which involves taking the tea leaves and boiling it in 2 cups of water for 5 - 10 minutes, then strain to remove the tea leaves. This mixture should sit for a while to cool before being added to the final beverages. While it is cooling, prepare the rest.

2. Boil the ½ cup of tapioca pearls in 4 cups of water until soft for 20 minutes. Strain the tapioca pearls and discard this water.
3. Move the tapioca pearls from the sieve to a bowl and add the brown sugar. Then pour on 1 cup of hot water. Mix well to ensure the brown sugar dissolves. Then let it sit for 25 minutes giving the mixture an occasional stir.
4. Remove the tapioca balls using the sieve which will leave behind the brown sugar syrup which has

marinated in the tapioca pearls. This will be used to add sweetness to the beverage.
5. Transfer the tapioca balls into 2 glasses, evenly, then add a $1/2$ cup of ice to each drinking glass. Then add the brown sugar syrup according to your taste preference.
6. Add the cooled black tea to the glasses equally, (approx. 1 cup each), then a $1/4$ cup of milk to each glass. Add a large wide straw to extract the tapiocas up. Stir and enjoy.

## LEMON & GREEN ICED TEA

Ingredients (serves 6)
5 Tablespoons of Green tea            2 Lemons
2 Tablespoons Golden Caster Sugar     10 Mint Leaves
1 Tablespoon of Honey                 3 Cups of Ice

Instructions

1. Boil the green tea leaves in 1.5 litres of water in a pan for 10 minutes.
2. Juice one lemon and add the juice to the mixture. For the other lemon, slice it and add it to the pot. Add the honey and mint leaves. Taste the mixture and add more sugar/honey to taste preference.
3. Simmer for 5 - 7 minutes, then remove the pan from the heat.
4. Strain the green tea leaves & let the mixture cool.
5. Prepare the glasses with ice and pour in the mixture. Enjoy this simple but refreshing lemon green tea!

## KOMBUCHA TEA (CHINA)

Kombucha is very popular at the moment. This drink is slightly alcoholic and requires a SCOBY which is a Symbiotic Culture of Bacteria & Yeast!

Ingredients
6 Teaspoons of Black or Green Tea leaves
16 Cups of Water
1 Cup of Sugar
Kombucha Scoby (see pic) (These can be bought or made)
2 Cups of Kombucha Tea Starter Liquid (can be bought unflavoured)

Instructions

1. Make the sweet tea. Boil the water with tea leaves for 15 minutes and add sugar. Then, strain out the tea leaves and leave the tea to cool.
2. Add the scoby and the tea mixture to a **large** glass jar. Push the scoby to the bottom of the jar using a spoon and add the starter liquid culture as well. Ensure the tea mixture is just below room temperature before adding.
3. Cover with a cloth and rubber band and let it be stored away from sunlight for around 7 - 30 days in a temperature of 25 – 29 °C.
4. Do a taste test every day until perfect. If the mixture is still too sweet, it's not ready. If it is too

# CHAPTER 7: FORTY RECIPES FOR TEA

sour, then it is overdone. You want it somewhere in between. It should be pleasantly tangy & fizzy.

5. Then, when ready, you can remove the scoby & take out the first 2 cups. These first 2 cups will become your starter liquid for the next batch you make. Store this appropriately. Then you want to grab some bottles & add in your flavourings to the bottles e.g., berries, lemons etc to the bottle. Then, bottle the kombucha tea liquid & store in your fridge. Reused glass bottles are preferrable to buying new. Making big batches of Kombucha is also a good idea as it takes at least a week to be ready. Enjoy this mildly alcoholic kombucha iced tea at your own desire!

## TEA INFUSED WINE

Black and Oolong work best for red wine, but for white wine, you can use green, white, oolong and black tea.

Ingredients
1 Bottle of Your Favourite Wine
5 Tablespoons of Tea Leaves
Hot Water

Instructions

1. Rinse Tea leaves in hot water to start infusion process.
2. Decant the wine into a large jug. Add the tea leaves.

3. If white wine, store in fridge for 8-12 hours with cover. If red wine, store at room temp covered for a similar amount of time.
4. Strain out the tea leaves and put the tea infused wine back in its original bottle. Serve and enjoy! This can be enjoyed cold or just below room temp.

## RASPBERRY ICED TEA

Enjoy this refreshing summer beverage when you have guests over!

<u>Ingredients</u>  (serves 16)
4 Litres of Water
10 Tablespoons of Green Tea Leaves
Ice Cubes
350g of Frozen Raspberries
(1.5 - 2 Cups)
1½ Cups of Sugar
2 Lemons
Several Fresh Raspberries for Jug

<u>Instructions</u>

1. Juice 1 lemon to obtain at least a ¼ Cup of Lemon Juice.
2. Heat up the water and add sugar and mix until dissolved. Add raspberries and tea and lemon juice. Bring this to just below boiling then put on low heat for 10 minutes.

3. Strain the tea bags out and the frozen raspberries. Let the liquid cool.
4. After this transfer into a large jug, with ice. Garnish with fresh raspberries. Cut the second lemon up into slices and add to the pitcher. Add mint leaves as an optional extra. Add extra sugar to taste preference, serve & enjoy.

## RHUBARB MINT TEA

<u>Ingredients</u>  (serves 6)
2 Cups of Fresh, Chopped Rhubarb (frozen can be used too)
1 Cup of Fresh Raspberries (frozen can be used too)
Ice Cubes
1.5 Litres of Water (6½ Cups)
3 Tablespoons of Green Tea Leaves
½ Cup of Sugar (to taste)
11 g of Mint Leaves (0.4 ounces)
6 Mint Sprigs

<u>Instructions</u>

1. Add the water, fruit, mint leaves & sugar together in a pot and bring to boil, then simmer on low heat for 15 minutes. 5 minutes in to simmering add the tea leaves for the last 10 minutes. Then after this, strain the mixture and leave to cool.
2. Serve the mixture in glasses with ice and add 1 mint sprig to each glass.

## WHITE ICED TEA

**Ingredients** (serves 6)
11 Mint Sprigs
1 Sliced Lemon
Ice Cubes
3 Tablespoons of Honey
4 Tablespoons of White Tea Leaves

**Instructions**

1. Add the water, white tea, 5 mint sprigs & honey to preference together in a pot and bring to boil, then simmer on low heat for 10-12 minutes. Then strain the mixture into a pitcher with some ice cubes and lemon slices and leave to cool.
2. Serve in glasses with ice and lemon slices and 1 mint sprig per glass. Enjoy!

## TEA BLENDS

### Your own Black Tea Blend

English Breakfast tea is traditionally a blend of Assam black tea & Darjeeling black tea. If you are growing your own tea, you could try blending some purchased Assam or Darjeeling black tea leaves with your own grown black tea leaves and see how the combination fairs to the taste! Another common combination is with Ceylon black tea. Vary the ratio of each of the teas you experiment with until you are happy and know your own preference. Store them in labelled jars, so you know which ratio & blend is associated with which taste. If, after experimenting, your tea blend has a unique taste that is different to other blends out there, consider creating your own speciality tea brand (if you produce enough to sell). Start by introducing others to your tea blend and getting live feedback. Other common ingredients to add to black tea: citrus fruit peel, vanilla pods, cinnamon, cardamom, cloves, & ginger etc.

### Your own Oolong Tea Blend

Why not purchase a few different varieties of famous oolong and see how they pair with your home-made oolong tea? Always label & trial. You could for example trial Dan Cong, the Iron Goddess of Mercy or Da Hong Pao, all of which have been mentioned in the book prior. Finding out if you prefer Chinese grown, Indian grown, Sri-Lankan grown, or Kenyan grown tea is key to knowing which teas will combine well with yours according to your preference. You may not like the tea you have grown, but hope is not lost. This makes it an even better idea to combine it with ones you do like, so your hard work does not go to waste.

### Russian Caravan Tea Blend

Russian caravan tea is a blend of Keemun Black Tea, Lapsang Souchong Black Tea and Oolong Tea. To create this at home you could use the black tea you have processed in place of the Keemun and use the fourth leaf (souchong) of the tea and create a black lapsang souchong and finally the Oolong tea you have produced. Combine these in equal quantity to create this smoky flavoured tea blend. Alternatively, if you've only produced 1 or 2 of the 3, you can buy the others & blend them with the ones you've managed to grow & process.

## Your own Green Tea Blends

Add green teas together as with black tea and store. Make sure you label things to find out what works and what doesn't. Alternatively, you may want to add foreign green teas to your homegrown and processed green tea and then grind this blend into a matcha powder. This will really mix the flavours well and will be a unique product.

## Your own Green & Black Tea Blend

Some companies offer a green & black tea bag in one offering which is something you can easily recreate yourself. Initially try 50|50 black - green, then 60 | 40 & 40 | 60 and see which version you prefer. Reiterate the process until the ratios are perfect to your preference.

# CHAPTER 7: FORTY RECIPES FOR TEA

### Your own 2 Season Blend

Often the 1st and 2nd season's harvest are associated with quality, yet they have different taste attributes. Some companies offer a double season blend of the 1st and 2nd season's harvest from Darjeeling or Assam. You may even find some companies offering a combination of the two. Why not try blending your first & second flush tea harvest to see if it elevates the taste experience. If the taste is unique & offers something enjoyable that is different from drinking the tea from each flush individually, then keep blending & refining the quantities over time.

### Tea Blends from Multiple Cultivars

As with all the tea blends suggested above, if you have planted multiple cultivars in your tea nursery, it is worth combining tea harvested from the different cultivars to see the effects on the tea's taste. For example, one with more antioxidants with one that has lower caffeine content.

## FOOD RECIPES

Even if you have had success with your tea growing and harvesting journey, it does not necessarily mean your grown tea will immediately be more enjoyable than your favourite tea brands. However, I certainly hope you get to a point where it is! Whatever happens don't let your tea go to waste. Even if you don't enjoy your home tea blends or the hot or iced tea it makes, try using your tea in food recipes too. Here are several easy food recipes with tea.

TRADITIONAL CHINESE MARBLE TEA EGGS (CHINA)

Ingredients
6 -7 eggs

Sauce ingredients:
4 Cups of water or 950 mL (~ 1 L)
1 Tablespoon of Black tea leaves
1.5 Tablespoon Oolong tea leaves
3/4 Cinnamon stick
2 Star anise
3 Tablespoons of soy sauce
1 Tablespoon of sugar
0.5 Tangerine Peel (soak peel in water before use),
1 Teaspoon of salt (add more to taste)

Instructions

1. Boil eggs in room temperature water that covers at least 1 inch above the eggs, with the lid off in medium - high heat until you bring the water to boil. Then, on low heat, replacing the pot lid,

simmer for 1 minute. Remove from heat, & with the lid on, let it sit for 10 minutes.
2. Transfer eggs to cold water until you can pick them up easily.
3. While eggs are cooling, put the remaining ingredients in a saucepan to be heated together.
4. Use a needle to poke lightly a few times around the shell for better colouring & flavouring of eggs or lightly crack the shell all over. Removal of shells from the eggs happens right as you eat them.
5. Place the eggs in the sauce & ensure completely covered in the sauce. If you pierce the eggs with a needle, it will allow the flavours to seep through the egg. Bring sauce to boil then cook in the sauce on low heat for 15 minutes.
6. Sieve the tea leaves out of the sauce, then cook the ingredients for 5 more minutes with the lid on.
7. Remove from heat without removing the lid. Let the eggs sit in the sauce for around 2-3 hours. In this period stir the mixture every so often to ensure even distribution of flavour. Heat the mixture before eating. (Resting period is according to preferred strength of taste)
8. Reheat, Remove the eggs from the sauce, remove the shell from the egg and enjoy! Store in an airtight container for 3-4 days max if not being consumed that day. Always heat the eggs up before eating.

## OOLONG TEA CAKE

<u>Ingredients</u> (serves 8)
½ Cup of Oolong Tea Leaves
1 Cup of Brown Sugar
½ Teaspoon of Vanilla Extract
3 Eggs
2 Blocks of Salted Butter (add salt if using unsalted)
2 Cups of Self Raising flour
1 Cup of Buttermilk
1 Teaspoon of Baking Powder
6 Cloves
1 Teaspoon of Cinnamon Powder
½ Teaspoon of Nutmeg Powder

<u>Instructions</u>

1. Preheat the oven to 350°F or 180°C. Use medium sized cake pan and butter it with some of the salted butter. Alternatively use parchment paper to line it.
2. Melt the butter in a pan and add the oolong tea into the pan. Simmer the mixture on low heat for 10 minutes. Remove it from the heat and let it sit for 5 minutes. The tea flavours need to diffuse into the butter.
3. Strain the butter through a sieve to remove the tea leaves.
4. Put the butter in the freezer for 15 minutes until it becomes a soft butter. You don't want it to go hard.

# CHAPTER 7: FORTY RECIPES FOR TEA

5. Place in a mixer for 2 minutes using the paddle attachment on medium speed. If you don't own a mixer, do this using a paddle by hand for 5-7 minutes. Add the 3 eggs to the mixer. If doing by hand, whisk the eggs before adding. Add the brown sugar after this.
6. Combine the flour, baking powder, salt, cloves, nutmeg, and cinnamon in a large bowl. Mix the ingredients together.
7. Add half the flour mix bit by bit to the butter/egg mix in the machine, make sure it is on a low-speed setting. Ensure it has mixed before adding more.
8. Add half the buttermilk to the mixer or mix it in by hand.
9. Add the rest of the flour mix & the vanilla extract. Let it mix thoroughly.
10. Finally add the remaining butter milk to the mixture. Mix this in again.
11. Once fully mixed, add the batter to the cake tray and bake for 45-50 minutes at the preheated temperature. Check the cake is ready by using a knife to pierce the cake. It should come out clean when ready.
12. Once ready remove and let it sit for at least 10 minutes before serving.

## MATCHA CHEESECAKE

<u>Ingredients</u> (serves 6)
100g Chocolate Digestive Biscuits
(Dark chocolate is preferrable)
¼ Cup of Cocoa Powder
50g Butter
6g Gelatin
200g cream cheese
100g Yogurt
60g Sugar
200g Whipping Cream
7g Matcha
20mL of Hot Milk
25mL of Water
¾ Teaspoon of Vanilla Extract (optional)

<u>Instructions</u>

1. Smash the chocolate digestive biscuits in a plastic sandwich bag to contain the crumbs. Ensure it becomes like a powder. Alternatively, use a food processor.
2. Melt the butter and mix it in a bowl with biscuits and cocoa powder until it's all wet and mixed.
3. Put the melted butter biscuits in a cake tin as a base and press it down until the base is firm. A tall 15 cm to 16 cm tin is fine.
4. Refrigerate the cake tin with biscuit base for 25 minutes.
5. Mix the 6g of gelatin with 25 mL of water. Let it sit for 15 minutes.

6. Mash the cream cheese until smooth and whisk it using silicone spatula or whisk until light. Then add the yogurt and sugar, then mix ingredients together. Add a spoon of vanilla extract here as well.
7. Melt the gelatin by putting the bowl you sat for 15 minutes in another bowl of hot water, then mix it until it turns liquid again. Add this to the cream cheese mixture and mix.
8. Take the whipping cream and whisk for 5-10 minutes then add to the cheese mixture and mix. Take out the cake tin and add half the mixture spreading it evenly in the tin. Put this in the freezer for 20 mins.
9. Add the 7 grams of matcha powder to 20mL of hot milk and mix thoroughly into a paste and let it cool on the counter.
10. Once cooled, add to the second half of the cream cheese mixture, & thoroughly mix until green through. Take the cake out the freezer & add the matcha mix to the top of the cream cheese & spread evenly.
11. Refrigerate for 3 - 3.5 hours then cut up and enjoy!

## JAMAICAN FISH TEA SOUP WITH TEA

Despite the dish's name, this Jamaican recipe does not normally have any tea in it. However, this modified version below does include tea.

<u>Ingredients</u> (serves 6)
1 Scotch Bonnet (diced)
3 Tablespoons of Green or Black Tea Leaves
2 Cloves of Garlic or 2 Teaspoons of Garlic Paste
Fresh Thyme (Small Handful)
2 Large White Onions (Finely Diced)
1 Large Carrot (Peeled & Diced)
2 Celery Sticks (Diced)
2 Cups of Baby Potatoes (Chop each potato in half)
1 lb of Prawns (0.5 kg)
8 Cups Water with Fish Stock Cubes
1 lb of White Fish (0.5 kg) (Cut into medium sized chunks)
Coriander leaves & Lemon Slices to Garnish

<u>Instructions</u>
1. Heat some olive oil in a pan and fry the onions. cook until the onions turn fully brown. Then add the diced carrots & celery plus a pinch of salt & pepper. Cook for about 3 minutes.
2. Add garlic, thyme & the scotch bonnet to the pan & keep frying.
3. Simultaneously, in another pan bring the 8 cups of water with fish stock cubes to boil. Add the tea

leaves, then let it simmer on low heat for 10-15 minutes. Then strain out the tea leaves.
4. Add the potatoes and the prawns. Fry for 1 minute to get the flavour onto the prawns. Then transfer this pans contents carefully to the fish stock pan and add the white fish. Let the contents simmer for 20 minutes. Squeeze in a little lemon juice.
5. Add salt and pepper to season to preference, until satisfied with the taste. Then serve into the bowls. Garnish the soup with coriander leaves and a slice of lemon to supplement the fish flavours.

## GREEN TEA CHICKEN NOODLE SOUP

<u>Ingredients</u> (serves 8)
6 Cups of Water
1 Packet of Chicken Broth
3 Tablespoons of Green Tea Leaves
2 Chicken Breasts, Cooked & Shredded
2 Cups of Dry Egg Noodles
2 Tablespoons Extra-Virgin Olive Oil
2 Cups of Mushrooms, Washed & Finely Diced
2 Yellow Onion, Diced
1 Teaspoon of Dried Basil
2 Carrots, Peeled and Diced
1 Cup of Frozen or Canned Sweetcorn
3 Cloves of Garlic, Minced
2 Tablespoons of Freshly Grated Ginger
Cup of Diced Green Onions
$1/4$ Cup of Chopped Cilantro
Salt & Pepper to Season to Preference

## Instructions

1. Use 3 cups of water to make the green tea. Bring the tea to boil then simmer on low heat for 10 minutes. Then strain the green tea leaves out.
2. Make the chicken broth according to the packet with the remaining 3 cups of water in another pot. *(You can also use 1-2 chicken stock cubes instead).*
3. In a third much larger pot, sauté the yellow onions and carrots together with oil and season with salt and pepper. When the onions start to turn brown, add the mushrooms, sweetcorn, ginger, and garlic and keep on heat while mixing for 7 minutes. Add the basil at the end of the 7 minutes.
4. Next add the egg noodles, the chicken broth, and the green tea to the large pot. Let the chicken soup simmer on low heat for a good 30 minutes at least to allow all the flavour to diffuse. Season with salt and pepper accordingly.
5. About 15 minutes into simmering, add in your pre-cooked & shredded chicken into the soup. This can be pre-fried or baked according to preference.
6. Season with cilantro and green onion to finish. Then serve and enjoy!

---

### EARL GREY SHORTBREAD COOKIES

Ingredients (24 Cookies)
2 Cups of Self Raising Flour
2 Tablespoons of Earl Grey Tea (Either made by yourself or purchased)
$3/4$ Teaspoon of Orange Zest

½ Teaspoon of Lemon Zest
Alternatively, if you don't have any Earl Grey, use Black tea, as the orange and lemon zest will simulate Earl Grey flavours.
1 Teaspoon of Vanilla Extract
¾ Cup of Confectioners' Sugar
1 Cup of Salted Butter (soft)
(Add ½ Teaspoon of Salt if using unsalted butter)
¼ Cup of Water or Milk

Instructions

1. In a food processor blend the flour, tea, salt until fine. If you are using your own made earl grey tea leaves, consider washing the leaves in boiling water first. This will start tea diffusion and kill off any germs.
2. Add the vanilla extract, orange & lemon zest, butter and sugar and blend in the processor until the dough is formed. If the dough appears too dry, add a little water or milk to help stick everything together and process again until the dough is perfect. Then, remove & roll the dough into a log shape of a diameter of about 5 - 7 cm, cover it and put in the fridge for 30 minutes.
3. Preheat the oven to 375°F or 190°C.
4. Take out the dough from the fridge and slice the log in to thin 1 cm thick slices. These will be your

cookies. Place these on a baking tray with a baking sheet on the bottom
5. Bake in the oven for 10 minutes and check the progress. Likely they will need another 5-7 minutes. Make sure the top is just turning a light brown colour.
6. Take them out the oven when ready, let them cool, then enjoy!

---

## MATCHA CHOCOLATE CHIP PANCAKES

Ingredients (serves 4)

2 Teaspoons of Matcha Powder 100mL of Milk
200g of Self Raising Flower
1 Teaspoon of Baking Powder
2 Tablespoons of Maple Syrup
$1/2$ Teaspoon of Vanilla Extract
3 Eggs
35g Butter
25g of Chocolate Chips

# CHAPTER 7: FORTY RECIPES FOR TEA

<u>Instructions</u>

1. Mix the Matcha powder and milk well.
2. Mix the flour and baking powder in a large bowl.
3. Melt 25g of butter and add the maple syrup and vanilla extract. Add these to the flour and mix thoroughly.
4. Add the matcha milk mix and finally, the chocolate chips. The mixture should be fluid and if it is not, supplement with more milk.
5. Finally, having mixed all the ingredients together, butter a frying pan with the remaining butter (use as required) and begin frying your pancakes.
6. If you want to get a thicker pancake with a smaller diameter, you can either use a very small frying pan (e.g., 1 egg frying pan) or place a small cake tin or cookie cutter shape on the frying pan and pour a bit of the mixture into it. Press down the tin/cutter to ensure the batter doesn't leak. You can remove hand when it has cooked enough to retain its own shape then remove cake tin/cookie cutter and flip the pancake. Cook the full batch the same & enjoy!

## SWEET TEA FRIED CHICKEN

### Ingredients

**Chicken Batter**
5 Chicken Legs with skin
5 Chicken Thighs bone & skin
2 Cups of Buttermilk
1- 2 Tablespoon of Sriracha (to preference)
3 Cups of Flour
1 Cup of Cornmeal
2 Tablespoons of Corn Starch
2 Teaspoons of Garlic powder
1 ½ Teaspoons of Black pepper
1 ½ Teaspoons of salt
½ Teaspoon of Cayenne Pepper
½ Tea spoon of Paprika (can use smoked too)

**Sweet Tea Marinade**
6 Tablespoons of Black, Green or White Tea
6 Cups of Water
1 Cup of White Sugar
¼ Cup of Salt

**Frying**
3 - 4 Cups of Vegetable Oil for Deep Frying

### Instructions

1. Make the sweet tea. Bring the water to boil and add the tea leaves in the water for around 20 minutes on simmer when it reaches boiling. Add the sugar & salt. Then remove from the heat & strain the tea leaves. Let the mixture cool to room temp covered for an hour or so.
2. Take the chicken pieces and put them in freezer bags and fill the bags with the sweet tea which

should be at room temperature. Let them marinade in the fridge for 24 hours at least.
3. Prepare the batter by combining the remaining powder ingredients.
4. Remove the chicken and add the sriracha to the batter.
5. Pour the butter milk into a separate bowl. Cover the chicken completely in the flour batter.
6. Heat up the oil in a wok for a while or heat up the oil in a deep fryer. Then fry the chicken until golden brown. About 8 minutes.
7. Remove the chicken. The legs will likely be done but you need to check the thigh are cooked through. If not, finish off in the oven for 15 minutes at 180°C.

## FINAL REMARKS

Thank you for joining me on this tea growing journey. I hope you have found the book useful and informative. Here's a quick recap on what we have covered. Initially I defined tea and what <u>doesn't</u> classify as tea looking at the 6 types of tea that exist and the different types of plants used for herbal & fruit infusions. We then looked at the 6 main ways to determine quality in tea including Processing Technique, Tea Grade, Leaf Size, Flush, Cultivar & Region. We went on a journey around the world exploring the various teas, tea blends, infusions, & creations from around the world. We then looked at how to <u>plant</u> tea, <u>prune</u> it and maintain it from tea seeds, cuttings, to seedlings and how to <u>harvest</u> & <u>process</u> the tea for each of the 6 major types of tea. We even looked at how you can make your own <u>decaffeinated</u> tea at home should you prefer it. No matter the climate you are in, there is a way to grow tea. Even in extreme climates & unfavourable conditions, I hope you now have an idea of how you might accomplish tea growth. You should now know some of the pests you will encounter, the tea diseases your plant may suffer and how basic cultivation works. And at last, I hope these 40 different recipes listed in this final chapter will be of use to you. Even if you try 1 or 2, it will ensure your newly grown tea is put to good use.

# CHAPTER 7: FORTY RECIPES FOR TEA

If you are new to growing things, both in your garden or even pots indoors, consider growing vegetables next. I have a book that looks at the basics of self-sufficiency and how to become independent from the 'system' of today. A part of this is being able to live off the land. Growing your vegetables is a good way create variety in your garden which will minimise pests and diseases. Growing a variety of herbs is another way to keep those pests away too; So, don't forget to grab the freebie on page 7 if you are looking to get stuck into self-sufficiency and growing fruit, veg & herbs. We also have a Facebook group which you can join to share your journey with other like-minded individuals. See the link below:

https://www.facebook.com/groups/841837163138658

Please leave a review (**just scan QR Code**)

Finally, I would ask that if you enjoyed this book that you would leave me a review on Amazon or Goodreads as this will help me out a lot and will help others to find the book more easily!

201

# REFERENCES

1. Mate (HS: 090300) Product Trade, Exporters and Importers | OEC [Internet]. OEC - The Observatory of Economic Complexity. 2021 [cited 31 October 2021]. Available from: https://oec.world/en/profile/hs92/mate-2090300

2. What is Cacao Husk Tea? — The Husk Mill [Internet]. The Husk Mill. 2021 [cited 31 October 2021]. Available from: https://www.thehuskmill.com.au/about-our-teas

3. Wise G, Negrin A. A critical review of the composition and history of safe use of guayusa: a stimulant and antioxidant novel food. 2021.

4. Green Gold: Making Money (and Fighting Deforestation) with Yerba Mate [Internet]. Harvard International Review. 2020 [cited 31 October 2021]. Available from: https://hir.harvard.edu/green-gold-yerba-mate/

5. Mangan A. Restoring the Ecology and Culture of the Atlantic Forest with Yerba Mate - Bioneers [Internet]. Bioneers. [cited 31 October 2021]. Available from: https://bioneers.org/restoring-the-ecology-and-culture-of-the-atlantic-forest-with-yerba-mate-zmbz2106/?mc_cid=233b2bc0d0&mc_eid=b3db1e6983

6. Pardau M, Pereira A, Apostolides Z, Serem J, Bester M. Antioxidant and anti-inflammatory properties ofIlex guayusatea preparations: a comparison toCamellia sinensisteas [Internet]. 2017 [cited 31 October 2021].

Available from: https://pubmed.ncbi.nlm.nih.gov/29134218/

7. What is cascara? - Caffè Nero [Internet]. UK. [cited 31 October 2021]. Available from: https://caffenero.com/uk/the-journal/what-is-cascara/

8. Baladi E. Interesting story of yerba mate tea in Syria - Enab Baladi [Internet]. Enab Baladi. 2020 [cited 31 October 2021]. Available from: https://english.enabbaladi.net/archives/2020/01/interesting-story-of-yerba-mate-tea-in-syria/

9. Heaney S, Koidis T, Morin J. Tea and flavoured tea. FI Handbook on Food Authenticity Issues and Related Analytical Techniques [Internet]. 2018 [cited 31 October 2021];:315 - 334. Available from: https://secure.fera.defra.gov.uk/foodintegrity/index.cfm?sectionid=83

10. Health Benefits of Blood Oranges [Internet]. WebMD. [cited 1 November 2021]. Available from: https://www.webmd.com/diet/health-benefits-blood-oranges#1

11. Breus M. 8 Surprising Health Benefits of Nettle Tea [Internet]. The Healthy. 2021 [cited 1 November 2021]. Available from: https://www.thehealthy.com/home-remedies/nettle-tea-benefits/

12. Red Rose Tea: A History of a Classic [Internet]. redroseteaca-en. 2019 [cited 1 November 2021].

Available from: https://www.redrosetea.ca/a-history-of-a-classic

13. Cocoa shells, husks, skins and waste (HS: 180200) Product Trade, Exporters and Importers | OEC [Internet]. OEC - The Observatory of Economic Complexity. 2019 [cited 1 November 2021]. Available from: https://oec.world/en/profile/hs92/cocoa-shells-husks-skins-and-waste

14. Moura R, Resende A. Cardiovascular and Metabolic Effects of Açaí, an Amazon Plant. Journal of Cardiovascular Pharmacology [Internet]. 2015 [cited 1 November 2021];:24. Available from: https://www.researchgate.net/publication/286767042_Cardiovascular_and_Metabolic_Effects_of_Acai_an_Amazon_Plant

15. Keemun Black Tea Information and Brewing Tips – teavivre [Internet]. Teavivre.com. [cited 2 November 2021]. Available from: https://www.teavivre.com/info/general-information-about-keemun-black-tea.html

16. Keemun: The Smoky and Floral Chinese Black Tea [Internet]. Sencha Tea Bar. 2020 [cited 2 November 2021]. Available from: https://senchateabar.com/blogs/blog/keemun

17. Dr Sadik.D Chinese Dragon Tea: A Closer Look At Longjing Tea [Internet]. Tea Leafed. 2021 [cited 2 November 2021]. Available from: https://tealeafed.com/chinese-dragon-tea/

18. Hangzhou Attractions | Dragon Well Tea Village - History, location, tips & Transport [Internet]. Chinahangzhoutour.com. [cited 2 November 2021]. Available from: https://www.chinahangzhoutour.com/attractions/show/dragon_well_tea_plantation.htm

19. Darjeeling [Internet]. Teaboard.gov.in. 2021 [cited 2 November 2021]. Available from: http://www.teaboard.gov.in/TEABOARDCSM/NQ==

20. Xie J, Yu H, Song S, Fang C, Wang X, Bai Z et al. Pu-erh Tea Water Extract Mediates Cell Cycle Arrest and Apoptosis in MDA-MB-231 Human Breast Cancer Cells [Internet]. PubMed.GOV. 2017 [cited 2 November 2021]. Available from: https://pubmed.ncbi.nlm.nih.gov/28428754/

21. Zhao X, Qian Y, Zhou Y, Wang R, Wang Q, Li G. Pu-erh Tea Has In Vitro Anticancer Activity in TCA8113 Cells and Preventive Effects on Buccal Mucosa Cancer in U14 Cells Injected Mice In Vivo [Internet]. PubMed.GOV. 2014 [cited 2 November 2021]. Available from: https://pubmed.ncbi.nlm.nih.gov/24945996/

22. Zhao X, Song J, Kim J, Lee J, Park K. Fermented Pu-erh Tea Increases In Vitro Anticancer Activities in HT-29 Cells and Has Antiangiogenetic Effects on HUVECs [Internet]. PubMed.GOV. 2013 [cited 2 November 2021]. Available from: https://pubmed.ncbi.nlm.nih.gov/24579782/

23. Shoemaker S. Pu-erh Tea: Benefits, Dosage, Side Effects, and More [Internet]. Healthline. 2020 [cited 2

November 2021]. Available from: https://www.healthline.com/health/food-nutrition/pu-erh-tea-benefits#benefits-uses

24. About Pu-erh Tea [Internet]. The Chinese Tea Shop. [cited 2 November 2021]. Available from: https://thechineseteashop.com/pages/about-pu-erh-tea

25. What is Silver Needle White Tea? - The Daily Tea [Internet]. The Daily Tea. 2016 [cited 2 November 2021]. Available from: https://thedailytea.com/taste/elevation-silver-needle/

26. Kochman J, Jakubczyk K, Antoniewicz J, Mruk H, Janda K. Health Benefits and Chemical Composition of Matcha Green Tea: A Review [Internet]. US National Library of Medicine National Institutes of Health. 2020 [cited 2 November 2021]. Available from: https://www.ncbi.nlm.nih.gov/pmc/articles/PMC7796401/

27. Zhou Y, Liu X, Yang Z. Characterization of Terpene Synthase from Tea Green Leafhopper Being Involved in Formation of Geraniol in Tea (Camellia sinensis) Leaves and Potential Effect of Geraniol on Insect-Derived Endobacteria [Internet]. US National Library of Medicine National Institutes of Health. 2019 [cited 2 November 2021]. Available from: https://www.ncbi.nlm.nih.gov/pmc/articles/PMC6995508/

28. Higdon J. Tea [Internet]. Linus Pauling Institute. 2005 [cited 3 November 2021]. Available from: https://lpi.oregonstate.edu/mic/food-beverages/tea

29. How to Make Yellow Tea Like A Chinese Tea Master [Internet]. Sencha Tea Bar. 2020 [cited 3 November 2021]. Available from: https://senchateabar.com/blogs/blog/how-to-make-yellow-tea

30. Assam [Internet]. Teaboard.gov.in. 2021 [cited 3 November 2021]. Available from: http://www.teaboard.gov.in/TEABOARDCSM/Ng==

31. Hill A. Assam Tea: Nutrition, Benefits, and Precautions [Internet]. Healthline. 2020 [cited 3 November 2021]. Available from: https://www.healthline.com/nutrition/assam-tea

32. Wang L. Tea and Chinese Culture. 1st ed. San Francisco: Long River Press; 2005.

33. Gray A. The Little Tea Book. 1st ed. 2021.

34. Zheng X, Li Q, Xiang L, Liang Y. Recent Advances in Volatiles of Teas [Internet]. National Library of Medicine. 2016 [cited 4 November 2021]. Available from: https://www.ncbi.nlm.nih.gov/pmc/articles/PMC6273888/#B61-molecules-21-00338

35. García-Ruiz A, Baenas N, Benítez-González A, Stinco C, Meléndez-Martínez A, Moreno D et al. Guayusa (Ilex guayusa L.) new tea: phenolic and carotenoid composition and antioxidant capacity [Internet]. 2017 [cited 4 November 2021]. Available from: https://pubmed.ncbi.nlm.nih.gov/28188617/

36. Tie Guan Yin Iron Goddess of Mercy | Chinese Oolong Tea | Curious Tea [Internet]. Curious Tea. [cited 4 November 2021]. Available from: https://www.curioustea.com/tea/oolong-tea/tie-guan-yin-iron-goddess-of-mercy/

37. Sutcliffe T. The drink that costs more than gold [Internet]. Bbc.com. 2016 [cited 4 November 2021]. Available from: https://www.bbc.com/travel/article/20160425-the-pot-of-tea-that-costs-10000

38. Liu An Gua Pian - Teapedia [Internet]. Teapedia.org. 2013 [cited 4 November 2021]. Available from: https://teapedia.org/en/Liu_An_Gua_Pian

39. Junshan Yinzhen Tea, China Yellow Tea in Hunan - Easy Tour China [Internet]. Easytourchina.com. [cited 4 November 2021]. Available from: https://www.easytourchina.com/fact-v1268-junshan-yinzhen-tea

40. Sun B, Zhu Z, Cao P, Chen H, Chen C, Zhou X et al. Purple foliage coloration in tea (Camellia sinensis L.) arises from activation of the R2R3-MYB transcription factor CsAN1 [Internet]. Springer Nature Limited. 2016 [cited 4 November 2021]. Available from: https://www.nature.com/articles/srep32534

41. Will Purple Tea Become Our Climate Change Tea? [Internet]. Earth Buddies. [cited 4 November 2021]. Available from: https://earthbuddies.net/purple-tea/

42. Saak M. Differences between Orthodox and CTC teas [Internet]. Renegade Tea Estate. 2019 [cited 5 November 2021]. Available from: https://www.renegadetea.com/blogs/renegade-rumblings/differences-between-orthodox-and-ctc-teas

43. Sub-Sector Overview [Internet]. Naeb.gov.rw. 2019 [cited 5 November 2021]. Available from: https://naeb.gov.rw/index.php?id=44

44. Rooibos tea, the history & production - the Cederberg's secret ingredient [Internet]. Cederberg Ridge. 2018

[cited 5 November 2021]. Available from: https://cederbergridge.co.za/2019/10/02/history-of-rooibos-tea-industry/

45. Morton J. Rooibos tea,aspalathus linearis, a caffeineless, low-tannin beverage. Economic Botany. 1983;37(2):164-173.

46. Addis, W., 2020. *Discover Ethiopian Herbal Teas*. [online] Whatsoutaddis.com. Available at: <https://www.whatsoutaddis.com/2020/10/30/discover-ethiopian-herbal-teas/> [Accessed 5 November 2021].

47. Wu G, Sugimoto C, Kinjo H, Azama C, Mitsube F, Talon M et al. Diversification of mandarin citrus by hybrid speciation and apomixis [Internet]. Nature Communications. 2021 [cited 6 November 2021]. Available from: https://www.nature.com/articles/s41467-021-24653-0

48. Black Tea Orange Pekoe -Loose Leaf 100g | Gorreana Shop [Internet]. Gorreana. [cited 6 November 2021]. Available from: https://gorreana.pt/en/shop//orange-pekoe-loose-leaf-100g-18

49. Mehik K. Why did the Georgian tea industry collapse? [Internet]. Renegade Tea Estate. 2018 [cited 6 November 2021]. Available from: https://www.renegadetea.com/blogs/renegade-rumblings/why-did-the-georgian-tea-industry-collapse

50. Jafarova A. Ancient traditions of tea drinking in Azerbaijan [Internet]. AzerNews.az. 2013 [cited 6 November 2021]. Available from: https://www.azernews.az/culture/49831.html

51. Tea consumption per capita worldwide by country, 2016 | Statista [Internet]. Statista. 2016 [cited 6

November 2021]. Available from: https://www.statista.com/statistics/507950/global-per-capita-tea-consumption-by-country/

52. Zavarka Brewing: How to Make Tea Russian Style [Internet]. Tea Culture. 2017 [cited 6 November 2021]. Available from: https://tea-culture.net/zavarka-russian-tea/

53. Russian Caravan [Internet]. Twinings. [cited 6 November 2021]. Available from: https://twinings.co.uk/blogs/news/russian-caravan

54. The History Of Earl Grey Tea - Timeless Tea With a Colourful History | Madura Tea [Internet]. Madura Tea. 2018 [cited 8 November 2021]. Available from: https://www.maduratea.com.au/_c/talking-tea/earl-grey-tea-the-timeless-tea-with-a-colourful-history/

55. Yan Y, Jeong S, Park C, Mueller N, Piao S, Park H et al. Effects of extreme temperature on China's tea production [Internet]. Iopscience.iop.org. 2021 [cited 8 November 2021]. Available from: https://iopscience.iop.org/article/10.1088/1748-9326/abede6/pdf

56. Yan P, Wu L, Wang D, Fu J, Shen C, Li X et al. Soil acidification in Chinese tea plantations [Internet]. National Library of Medicine. 2020 [cited 8 November 2021]. Available from: https://pubmed.ncbi.nlm.nih.gov/32014781/

57. Yang S, Jiang C, Zhang Q. Effects of windbreaks on wind-decrease, temperature-increase and moisture content of tea leaves in tea garden [Internet]. RESEARCH GATE. 2010 [cited 10 November 2021]. Available from: https://www.researchgate.net/publication/293293367_

Effects of windbreaks on wind-decrease temperature-increase and moisture content of tea leaves in tea garden

58. Co. J. Matcha vs Sencha (Loose-leaf) Green Tea: What Are the Differences? [Internet]. Japanese Green Tea Co. 2021 [cited 11 November 2021]. Available from: https://www.japanesegreentea in.com/blogs/green-tea-and-health/matcha-vs-sencha-loose-leaf-green-tea-what-are-the-differences

59. Heathcote A. Timeline: A short history of Australian tea - Australian Geographic [Internet]. Australian Geographic. 2017 [cited 11 November 2021]. Available from: https://www.australiangeographic.com.au/topics/history-culture/2017/07/timeline-a-short-history-of-australian-tea/

60. Australian Tea [Internet]. Nerada Tea. [cited 11 November 2021]. Available from: https://neradatea.com.au/blogs/history/australian-tea

61. Kawakawa - the medicine plant. Waikato Regional Beachcare Magazine [Internet]. 2012 [cited 11 November 2021];(3):6. Available from: http://www.waikatoregion.govt.nz

62. Tea only Archives - Zealong Tea Estate [Internet]. Zealong Tea Estate. [cited 11 November 2021]. Available from: https://zealong.com/product-types/tea-only/

63. Escapee tea | The Cook and the Curator | Sydney Living Museums [Internet]. Blogs.sydneylivingmuseums.com.au. 2013 [cited 12 November 2021]. Available from:

https://blogs.sydneylivingmuseums.com.au/cook/escapee-tea/

64. Derraik J. New Zealand manuka (Leptospermum scoparium; Myrtaceae): a brief account of its natural history and human perceptions. New Zealand Garden Journal [Internet]. 2008 [cited 12 November 2021];11(2):4-8. Available from: https://www.rnzih.org.nz/RNZIH_Journal/Pages_4-8_from_2008_Vol11_No2.pdf

65. Patel P, Zhang D, Borthakur D, Hazarika M, Boruah P, Barooah R et al. Quality Green Tea (Camellia sinensis L.) Clones Marked through Novel Traits. Beverages [Internet]. 2019;5(4):63. Available from: https://www.researchgate.net/publication/336973802_Quality_Green_Tea_Camellia_sinensis_L_Clones_Marked_through_Novel_Traits

66. Cultivation of Japanese Green Tea [Internet]. O-cha.net. [cited 18 November 2021]. Available from: https://www.o-cha.net/english/cup/pdf/14.pdf

67. TEA HARVESTING SEASONS / DATES [Internet]. Estate Tea Co. [cited 18 November 2021]. Available from: https://estateteaco.co.uk/pages/tea-harvesting-seasons

68. Tea Seasons [Internet]. CTPE. [cited 18 November 2021]. Available from: https://ceylonteaplantation.com/ceylon-tea/tea-seasons/

69. Kamunya S, Ochanda S, Cheramgoi E, Chalo R, Sitienei K, Muku O et al. Tea Growers Guide. Kenya Agricultural & Livestock Research Organization [Internet]. 2019 [cited 18 November 2021];1(1):18, 1-50. Available from: https://www.kalro.org/sites/default/files/Tea_Growers

_Guide_for_Mobile_App_TRI_28_Feb_2019_SK_ed_LW.pdf

70. Seasonal Teas by Country / Type of Tea – Tea Trekker [Internet]. Teatrekker.com. [cited 18 November 2021]. Available from: https://www.teatrekker.com/seasonal-teas-by-country/

71. Waine T, Redfern S, Corstanje R, Snapir B. Harvest Monitoring of Kenyan Tea Plantations With X-Band SAR. IEEE Journal of Selected Topics in Applied Earth Observations and Remote Sensing [Internet]. 2018 [cited 18 November 2021];1(1):1-9. Available from: https://www.researchgate.net/publication/323371695_Harvest_Monitoring_of_Kenyan_Tea_Plantations_With_X-Band_SAR

72. Cowan-Gore I, Sein T. Myanmar Tea Cultivation and Processing Guide. STRENGTHEN Publication Series Guide 2020 [Internet]. 2020 [cited 18 November 2021];1(1):1-64. Available from: https://www.ilo.org/yangon/projects/strengthen/WCMS_742461/lang--en/index.htm

73. INFOCOMM. TEA: An INFOCOMM Commodity Profile [Internet]. 2016 p. 1-25. Available from: https://unctad.org/system/files/official-document/INFOCOMM_cp11_Tea_en.pdf

74. Jones S. Black Tea Leaf Grading [Internet]. 2009 [cited 19 November 2021]. Available from: https://commons.wikimedia.org/wiki/File:Black_tea_grading.jpg

75. Introduction to Tea Cultivars [Internet]. Tea in the City. 2017 [cited 19 November 2021]. Available from: https://teainthecity.com/blogs/news/what-is-a-tea-cultivar

76. Sabhapondit S, Karak T, Bhuyan L, Goswami B, Hazarika M. Diversity of Catechin in Northeast Indian Tea Cultivars. The Scientific World Journal [Internet]. 2012;2012:1-8. Available from: https://pubmed.ncbi.nlm.nih.gov/22448135/

77. Magoma G, Obanda M, Imbuga M, Agong S. The use of catechins as biochemical markers in diversity studies of tea (Camellia sinensis). Genetic Resources and Crop Evolution [Internet]. 2004 [cited 19 November 2021];47(2):107. Available from: https://www.deepdyve.com/lp/springer-journal/the-use-of-catechins-as-biochemical-markers-in-diversity-studies-of-aXcZzGojuB?key=springer

78. Gai Z, Wang Y, Jiang J, Xie H, Ding Z, Ding S et al. The Quality Evaluation of Tea (Camellia sinensis) Varieties Based on the Metabolomics. HortScience [Internet]. 2019 [cited 19 November 2021];54(3):409-415. Available from: https://journals.ashs.org/hortsci/view/journals/hortsci/54/3/article-p409.xml?ArticleBodyColorStyles=pdf-4377

79. Wei K, Wang L, Zhou J, He W, Zeng J, Cheng H et al. Catechin contents in tea ( Camellia sinensis) as affected by cultivar and environment and their relation to chlorophyll contents. Food Chemistry [Internet]. 2011 [cited 19 November 2021];125(1):44. Available from: https://www.researchgate.net/publication/248511439_Catechin_contents_in_tea_Camellia_sinensis_as_affected_by_cultivar_and_environment_and_their_relation_to_chlorophyll_contents

80. Han W, Li X, Yan P, Zhang L, Ahammed G. Global tea science. 1st ed. 2018.

81. Jolvis Pou K. Fermentation: The Key Step in the Processing of Black Tea. Journal of Biosystems

Engineering [Internet]. 2016 [cited 23 November 2021];41(2):85-92. Available from: https://www.researchgate.net/publication/309375687_Fermentation_The_Key_Step_in_the_Processing_of_Black_Tea

82. Zhang Y, Skaar I, Sulyok M, Liu X, Rao M, Taylor J. The Microbiome and Metabolites in Fermented Pu-erh Tea as Revealed by High-Throughput Sequencing and Quantitative Multiplex Metabolite Analysis. PLOS ONE [Internet]. 2016 [cited 23 November 2021];11(6). Available from: https://www.ncbi.nlm.nih.gov/pmc/articles/PMC4918958/

83. The Ultimate Guide to Aged Tea in 5 Minutes [Internet]. Mansa Tea. [cited 23 November 2021]. Available from: https://mansatea.com/blogs/learn/aged-tea

84. Production of Chinese Yellow Tea [Internet]. Chazhidao Chinese Tea Traditions School. [cited 23 November 2021]. Available from: https://chazhidao.org/en/fourth-circle/production-chinese-yellow-tea

85. Abbasi P, Riga E, Conn K, Lazarovits G. Effect of neem cake soil amendment on reduction of damping-off severity and population densities of plant-parasitic nematodes and soilborne plant pathogens. Canadian Journal of Plant Pathology [Internet]. 2005 [cited 24 November 2021];27(1):38-45. Available from: https://www.tandfonline.com/doi/abs/10.1080/07060660509507191

86. Calendula Tea: Are There Health Benefits? [Internet]. WebMD. [cited 24 November 2021]. Available from: https://www.webmd.com/diet/health-benefits-calendula-tea

87. 13 Plants That Repel Flies, Mosquitoes and Bugs | Eden Horticultural [Internet]. Eden Horticultural Blog -

Garden Design & Landscaping. [cited 24 November 2021]. Available from: https://edenhorticultural.co.uk/blog/plants-that-repel-flies-bugs/

88. Is Bt Safe for Humans to Eat? [Internet]. Entomological Society of America. 2018 [cited 24 November 2021]. Available from: https://www.entsoc.org/sites/default/files/files/Science-Policy/2018/ESA-Factsheet-Bt.pdf

89. Use This Vaseline Trick to Stop Aphid & Scale Pests Organically [Internet]. 2019 [cited 24 November 2021]. Available from: https://www.youtube.com/watch?v=iic-aHGhUb4

90. Rahman M, Hossain M, Das R, Ahmad I. Changes in Phytochemicals and Determination of Optimum Fermentation Time during Black Tea Manufacturing. Journal of Scientific Research [Internet]. 2020 [cited 26 November 2021];12(4):657-664. Available from: https://www.researchgate.net/publication/344977753_Changes_in_Phytochemicals_and_Determination_of_Optimum_Fermentation_Time_during_Black_Tea_Manufacturing

91. Shehasen M. Tea Plant (Camellia Sinensis) Breeding Mechanisms Role in Genetic Improvement and Production of Major Producing Countries. International Journal of Research Studies in Science, Engineering and Technology [Internet]. 2019 [cited 29 November 2021];6(11):10-20. Available from: https://ijrsset.org/pdfs/v6-i11/2.pdf

92. Vuong Q, Roach P. Caffeine in Green Tea: Its Removal and Isolation. Separation & Purification Reviews [Internet]. 2013 [cited 2 December 2021];43(2):155-174. Available from:

https://www.researchgate.net/publication/261550337_Caffeine_in_Green_Tea_Its_Removal_and_Isolation

93. The larva of the white beetle in the male hand. [Internet]. [cited 14 December 2021]. Available from: https://www.shutterstock.com/image-photo/larva-white-beetle-male-hand-1803198403

94. Abdull Razis A, Ibrahim M, Kntayya S. Health Benefits of Moringa oleifera. Asian Pacific Journal of Cancer Prevention [Internet]. 2014 [cited 17 December 2021];15(20):8571-8576. Available from: http://journal.waocp.org/article_29959_144683da90d0087df5c7b5ec76da5b57.pdf

95. Gopalakrishnan L, Doriya K, Kumar D. Moringa oleifera: A review on nutritive importance and its medicinal application. Food Science and Human Wellness [Internet]. 2016 [cited 17 December 2021];5(2):49-56. Available from: https://www.sciencedirect.com/science/article/pii/S2213453016300362

96. Serych J. File:Flower of camellia sinensis.jpg [Internet]. 2007 [cited 22 December 2021]. Available from: https://commons.wikimedia.org/wiki/File:Flower_of_camellia_sinensis.jpg

97. FULLY CHARGED SHOW. Sustainable City | Fully Charged [Internet]. 2017 [cited 28 December 2021]. Available from: https://www.youtube.com/watch?v=WCKz8ykyI2E

www.ingramcontent.com/pod-product-compliance
Lightning Source LLC
Chambersburg PA
CBHW072153100526
**44589CB00015B/2210**